LOOKING AFTER

CAGE BIRDS

LOOKING AFTER
CAGE BIRDS

DAVID ALDERTON

BLANDFORD

First published in this edition in 1995 by Blandford
A Cassell imprint
Cassell plc
Wellington House
125 Strand
London WC2R 0BB

Distributed in the United States
by Sterling Publishing Co. Inc.
387 Park Avenue South
New York, NY 10016–8810

Distributed in Australia by
Capricorn Link (Australia) Pty Ltd
2–13 Carrington Road, Castle Hill, NSW 2154

Text set Monotype Lasercomp Plantin 110
Printed and bound in Spain by Bookprint S.L.,
Barcelona

British Library Cataloguing in Publication Data
Alderton, David
    Looking after cage birds.
    1. Cage-birds
    I. Title
    636.6'86   SF461

    ISBN 0–7137–2578–8

Acknowledgments

The photographs in this book have been supplied by the following: Wilko Bergmans,
Bernsen's International Press Service Ltd, Zdenek Burian, Bruce Coleman Ltd, W.
de Grahl, J. Kenming, P. Leysen, A. van den Nieuwenhuizen, Popperfoto, Cees
Scholtz, Archiv Smeets, Pim Smit, Fotoarchiv Spaarnstadt, and P. Zwister.

Line diagrams drawn by George Thompson.

Contents

Introduction

Above Horus – the Falcon God here shown on a relief of the Egyptian King Wadfi dating back to 2900 BC, now in the Louvre at Paris.

Below An Egyptian drawing from 2750 BC, portraying a goose.

From the beginning of recorded history, birds have been closely associated with man, with past cultures leaving ample evidence of their affections for particular species. The South American Indians revered the Quetzal (*Pharomachrus mocinno*) as the God of the Air, taking the cock's ornate tail feathers for use in their ceremonies without ever killing a bird for the purpose. The Mayas subsequently adopted it into their culture, portraying it as the 'plumed serpent', the main god of the Toltec pantheon. Even today, the Quetzal still remains a national symbol for Guatemalans.

The Egyptians had close links with birds, which were reflected in their culture by the God Horus, which resembled a falcon. Geese also figured prominently in the murals of this period. Centuries later, in 1922 when Howard Carter was excavating the tomb of Tutankhamun, it was said that his pet Roller Canary fell victim to the alleged Curse of the Pharoahs. The bird was eaten by a cobra, which was regarded as a sacred

guardian of the dead king. This loss caused consternation among the native workers, and was investigated by an Egyptian official accompanied by a snake-charmer. The cobra re-appeared, and shortly afterwards, the official himself became ill and died.

While the Greeks kept parrots as pets, with Alexander the Great's name being given to the Alexandrine Parrakeet, the Romans brought Ring-necked Parrakeets back from Africa. These birds became so popular that they could command at least the price of a slave, and were housed in very expensive cages.

Parrots were first seen in Europe from the end of the fifteenth century. One Grey Parrot kept by Henry VIII, lived at Hampton Court Palace. Having called the boatman across the river, it then recommended to the king that the man received suitable payment for the journey by suggesting 'Give him a groat'. The association of Greys with royalty continued, and the pet kept by a mistress of Charles II was stuffed on its demise, and remains the oldest known example of avian taxi-dermy, being kept at Westminster Abbey in London.

Current trends

For many people today, mention of a pet bird immediately brings to mind a talking budgerigar or parrot, or perhaps even a singing canary. However, there are other species that will settle very well in a domestic environment. Many of these birds are colourful and lively, and are even quite talented songsters in some cases. Others will breed easily in the home, and watching the development of the resulting youngsters can provide hours of enjoyment. This book explores the whole field of keeping pet birds, along with some novel ideas on their accom-modation, apart from the use of standard cages. It aims to show that, with a little imagination and practicality, a natural setting, which is both decorative and functional within the home, can be provided for many species.

The supply of birds

While various species such as the Budgerigar and Zebra Finch are bred in very large numbers each year, some of the parrots and many finches and softbills kept as pets are im-ported from abroad. This trade in birds is regulated by the international CITES agreement. The use of air transportation has meant that birds can be moved rapidly and safely from one country to another, with tight regulations established to safe-guard their welfare in transit. They will then usually undergo

Page 7 African Grey Parrots (*Psittacus erithacus*) have been kept as pets for centuries. If obtained as youngsters, they can become very talented talkers.

a period of quarantine for several weeks, before they can be sold.

A certain section of opinion is opposed to this trade in birds, in spite of the much greater protection now afforded to endangered species by the licensing system. In many cases, with parrots in particular, if these were not sold to a dealer (having been caught and then exported), they would be eaten immediately as a source of protein. Faced with declining numbers of a species, it is easy to blame the trade in birds for the problem, but this is a gross over-simplification of a complex international situation.

Birds are imported almost exclusively from the less developed regions of the world, which are now under increasing pressure for economic reasons. The destruction of the birds' natural habitat, to provide timber and agricultural land, is the fundamental problem and continues unabated in many areas. Large numbers of birds are destroyed when they feed on the resulting crops. It is staggering that up to four million Red-billed Weavers (*Quelea quelea*) are destroyed annually in Africa for this reason.

It is encouraging, therefore, that a much greater number of species are being bred regularly in private collections, on a much wider scale than would be possible if such birds were confined exclusively to zoos. Indeed, the need of zoos to display their birds for viewing purposes is often not compatible with achieving the conditions necessary for breeding success. Some of the more progressive institutions, such as the superb Walsrode Bird Park in Germany, are now providing off-display aviaries exclusively for the breeding of rare species. Modern scientific aids are also being employed, with, for example, the use of incubators ensuring that parrots can be reared successfully by hand from the egg to maturity.

Much of this work has been undertaken privately by aviculturists without any official backing or recognition of their work. If through the keeping of a pet bird, others are drawn into this fascinating area of study, they will be assured of a life-long hobby.

Choosing a pet bird

Various guidelines in respect of a particular species are given in the relevant section, but overall, a bird should appear lively and alert, especially when someone is close at hand. Preening is a good sign of health, as is a bird which rests on one leg, with the other tucked in amongst its feathers. The plumage may appear tatty in the case of an imported bird, but given adequate care, this will generally be replaced by immaculate feathering

Page 10 A Red-billed Weaver or Quelea (*Quelea q. quelea*). Vast numbers of these birds are destroyed annually in Africa as pests.

Page 11 Preening is a sign of good health, as exemplified here by an Orange-cheeked Waxbill, (*Estrilda melpoda*).

at the next moult. The vent region ought not to be stained with droppings, while the nostrils should be of equal size.

For closer examination the bird must be taken out of its cage. When handling a bird, once the breast bone has been located, it is then possible to feel if there is a distinct hollow either side of it. This condition is referred to as 'going light', reflecting a weight loss which may result from a chronic disease.

It is not always possible to detect external parasites by sight, so purchasing a special safe aerosol to kill mites, available from many pet stores, is recommended. This will serve to eliminate any of these minute creatures from the outset, so they cannot cause any subsequent irritation to the bird.

1 Cages and flights

Adequate consideration must be given to the accommodation required, before deciding on a particular species. The provision of suitable housing can prove an expensive undertaking and may in fact turn out to be more costly than the bird itself in some cases. The cost of a cage, however, gives no indication of its suitability, and indeed, the ornate nature of many designs now being marketed detracts from their prime function, of allowing maximum flying space in a given area.

Basic rectangular designs are preferable, and the most spacious cage available should be chosen, ensuring that the spacing of the bars is not too wide for the species concerned. Finches, for example, will escape through the gaps in a cage intended for a parrot, while even a cockatiel may become stuck, or perhaps fall victim to a cat if it is able to put its head through the bars.

Cages are constructed using various materials, but those made of bamboo, designed in an oriental style, are not really functional, although they may appear decorative. They cannot be easily kept clean, which is always an important consideration, while most psittacines, even smaller species such as *Brotogeris* parrakeets, will rapidly destroy them by gnawing the bars away.

The most attractive and yet practical models now available are a combination of metal and plastic, and will suffice for the majority of species kept as pets, except the larger parrots which will destroy the plastic component. Such cages come in two parts, with the upper wire unit attaching to its plastic bottom by means of catches. It is therefore very simple to keep such cages clean, as the base can be washed off at frequent intervals. Budgerigar-type cages are made of more brittle plastic, and boiling water poured over the base is likely to cloud it, and may even crack it.

The major drawback of larger cages of this type, however, is also apparent when they are being cleaned, because the bird may slip out under the bottom as the base is being separated. The sliding tray present in smaller models is designed to prevent this difficulty, as it can also be positioned to form a

Bamboo cages should only be considered as ornaments, and not for housing birds.

Below right A modern budgerigar cage with a plastic base.

false floor to the wire unit before the two parts are separated, but this option is not available in all cases. A few designs do attempt to overcome the problem by introducing a cubic wire design, which simply fits into the plastic tray, but the wire on the floor rapidly becomes soiled, and is extremely difficult to clean off satisfactorily. The birds may also become trapped by their feet when walking on this floor, between the wire and plastic.

The bars on many cages have a chrome finish, which, if

treated carefully should not chip and then rust, but as an additional refinement, they may be treated with an epoxy resin, giving them a white appearance. This is non-toxic, and helps to increase the lifespan of the cage. Rusting cages are potentially dangerous, because as the bird climbs around the bars, in the case of budgerigars especially, they may ingest particles of rust, which cause crop irritation and damage. Verdigris associated with brass fitments in older parrot cages particularly, showing as a green surface deposit, is also likely to prove poisonous.

More traditional budgerigar and canary cages comprised of an all-metal framework, with plastic around the sides to reduce seed scattering, are quite suitable for such birds, but, with more crannies for dirt to accumulate in, these are often harder to keep clean. Those with bars running in a vertical direction used to be classed as budgerigar cages, whereas horizontal bars were considered more suitable for canaries, although this distinction is not really merited, as these birds do well in either type of cage.

Types of perch

Modern cages are often equipped with plastic perches. These are easy to remove and wash, helping to prevent foot infections from soiled perches, but they often appear uncomfortable for birds. Dowelling is still used in many cages, however, and unfortunately, as with the plastic, this is usually of a constant diameter. The bird always has to use the same part of its feet to grip the perch, and may well develop pressure sores as a result. These can become infected and progressively cripple the bird, especially in the case of bigger budgerigars. For all species, therefore, some attempt must be made to ensure that the perches are of variable shape and diameter.

Suitably-sized branches cut from fruit trees such as apple, or other safe woods such as sycamore, elder or ash are useful in this respect. As a guide, the perches should allow the bird to grip comfortably, being neither too large for it to grip, nor so small that the front toes curl round to touch the back claws. All perches used must be cut from trees which have not been treated with chemicals, a particular hazard in fruit-growing areas, and should be washed off before use in case they have been soiled by wild birds. Wooden perches of this type allow psittacines to gnaw and keep their beaks in trim. Such behaviour is quite normal, and it is extremely cruel, apart from the risk of causing feather-plucking, to deny parrots of all types access to such wood, even if in some cases, branches have to be renewed daily.

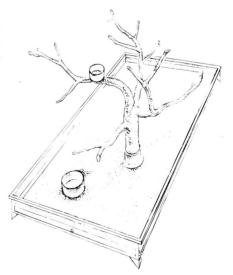

A suitable room perch for a tame parrot, set on a base which catches droppings and seed husks

By way of contrast, the smaller softbills will not destroy vegetation, and so benefit from the provision of growing plants in their enclosure, which are a more supple alternative to rigid perches. These birds are prone to foot disorders, which are much more easily prevented by this means than subsequently cured.

Cage stands

Stands to complement most cages are also available, and depending on the location chosen for the bird, a stand can be useful providing it is quite stable. With larger cages especially, it may be preferable to use a suitable piece of furniture instead, rather than risk both cage and stand being knocked over. This will apply when there is a boisterous dog in the household, for example, or young children, who may be seriously injured if they pull the stand over accidentally.

Points about cages for individual groups of birds

Pet budgerigars and canaries will thrive in standard cages, with modification to their perches, but those kept for breeding will require a more secluded environment. This is provided by means of a box-type cage described later, which is enclosed on all sides apart from the front, where the cage door is located.

Regrettably, parrots are still housed too often in small, square cages which are totally unsuited to their needs, allowing very little exercise so that ultimately the flight muscles will waste away, leaving the bird unable to fly any distance. A more flexible system, comprised of individual panels which clip together in any given combination thus giving the potential for a much larger cage, is available in some countries. Apart from benefiting the bird, these units are likely to be popular with pet store owners, as they require much less space for storage than a standard cage.

Parrot cages sometimes have a sheet-metal base which needs to be examined closely, to ensure that there are no gaps where a claw could be caught, as the sheet dents and distorts under very little pressure. Door catches are also inadequate in many instances, and are soon mastered by more intelligent birds. It may be necessary to use a padlock to overcome this fault, because a parrot loose in a room unaccompanied is a danger, both to itself and the fitments. In the case of cages for smaller birds, these usually close by means of a spring, and should only require some form of peg if this becomes inefficient.

Barrel-shaped upright cages marketed for finches could only have been designed by someone totally oblivious to the

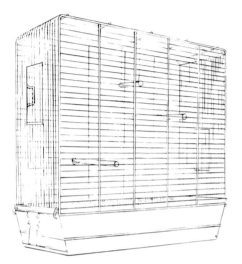

Typical modern cage designs

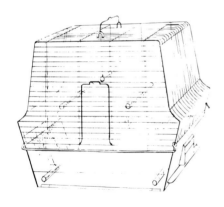

A parrot cage showing a cock cockatiel within. It is safer to remove the grid on the floor of such cages.

requirements of these active little birds. These designs should never be purchased. Such cages allow a bare minimum of flying-space, predominantly in a vertical direction, which is quite unnatural, as can be seen from watching such birds in an aviary, if not the wild. Although the larger budgerigar cages provide the most suitable accommodation for finches, the only real means of keeping them, so that their beauty can be fully appreciated, is to house them in a small flight or large wall cage. Such a structure will have to be specifically made, although this is not a difficult procedure. Such housing will also be required by most softbills, which, in view of their diet, are messy, so it is especially important that their accommodation can be both easily and thoroughly cleaned.

Mynah birds kept as pets are usually housed in box-type metal cages, in an attempt to prevent soiling of surrounding furniture, but these are far too small for their active natures. Consideration for the bird must rank above that of the owner, who can select another species should he not wish, or be able, to provide satisfactory accommodation. A mynah should not be expected to live in a cage less than 150 cm (5 ft) in length, and this applies to most other birds as well.

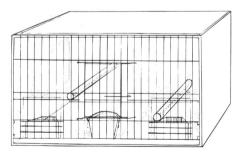

A box-type cage

Flight cages

These are the ideal means of maintaining a bird in the home, and with a little ingenuity, can be turned into decorative pieces of furniture. Cages are a useful adjunct, however, initially to get the bird tame and subsequently to act as a second home, if the flight is being repainted, for example. A simple flight also obviates the need to allow the bird exercise in the room, which is not an ideal environment in many cases, and prevents soiling as well as possible destruction of furniture.

Some firms, generally advertising in bird-keeping periodicals, produce complete indoor aviaries. Others sell wired panels, which can be assembled as required. The length of a flight as indicated is generally more significant than its height, although it must obviously have sufficient depth to allow the birds to fly without restriction. The structure should have a solid back, such as oil-tempered hardboard fixed on to a wooden frame, with wire panels forming the remainder of the structure apart from the base, which is usually also solid.

Before assembly, the component parts should be painted as desired, preferably with a light shade of emulsion. This paint is non-toxic, whereas any brand containing lead will result in poisoning if it is ingested. Some birds are naturally more destructive than others, and certain modifications to this design will be required for most psittacines, apart from budgerigars and cockatiels.

Most flight panels are made with 19 gauge wire, often abbreviated to 19G, which is not strong enough to retain such

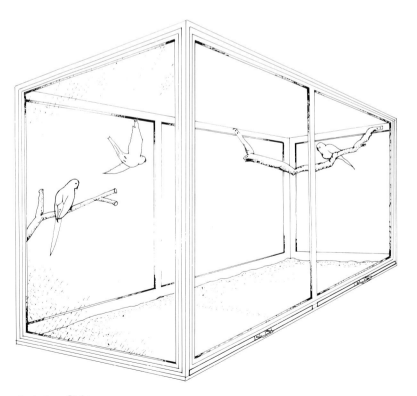

An indoor flight

parrots. Thicker 16G wire mesh will be necessary, and the framework will also need to be stouter, being constructed of 5cm (2in) square timber. Hardboard can still be used at the back of the structure, to prevent the wall becoming soiled, but all edges must be out of reach of the birds, because otherwise they will destroy this material without difficulty. Indeed, when the flight is finally assembled, all the woodwork should be on the outside, with its inner surface totally protected by wire. Exposed ends of cut netting are potentially dangerous, so they should either be filed down, having been made as short as possible, or bent over to the top of the frame, where they will be away from the birds when the flight is put together. Thin battening can also be nailed over loose ends as a protective measure, but this will attract the attention of parrot-like birds and, having been badly gnawed, may still permit injury.

At the front of the flight, a gap should be left between the base and the frame above, which must therefore be slightly shorter compared to the others in the unit. This allows a sliding tray to be inserted, fitting flush with the outer edge of the frame itself. The tray is simply constructed of hardboard, with strips of wood around the perimeter, corresponding to all the sides, which serve to retain the droppings and food debris more effectively. A handle on the front of the tray will facilitate its movement, with its actual height being determined by the species which will live in the flight. With the smaller birds, it should not be more than about 1.25cm (0.5in), as they will soon learn to escape underneath during cleaning.

A single small door positioned at the front of the flight, just above the tray, is generally most convenient. The bird can be fed through it, and caught without difficulty whenever necessary. It should therefore permit all corners of the cage to be reached comfortably, which also assists thorough cleaning. The door needs to be hinged and open outwards, with a suitable closing device, such as a sliding bolt, on the opposite side of the door to the hinges, not forgetting to protect any loose ends of netting as before.

The whole flight is most conveniently located on stout legs, which may themselves be mounted on castors, providing some form of braking system is fitted. This ensures that no dirt can accumulate around the base of the structure.

Attaching perches in an indoor flight

As in a cage, perches should run across the flight, rather than lengthways along it, to ensure that the birds have the maximum flying space. They can be fixed in place permanently by nails driven through the end of the branches at an angle, from the inside of the cage out through the hardboard to the framework. The sharp ends are then all out of the birds' reach if they chew the perch, and when sufficient of the nail protrudes, it can be knocked flat to give extra support. Netting staples offer the most straightforward means of attaching a perch to the netting at the front of the flight, and several spread the stress of the bird's weight when it lands on the perch. This will help to prevent the netting giving way around the staple, which is otherwise likely to occur, creating a hole in the process.

The smaller finches, such as waxbills, and some softbills, like Sugar Birds, are best housed with plants forming a significant proportion of the perches. A very attractive setting can soon be devised, and highlighted with a natural light bulb, which will be of benefit to the birds themselves. It is, however, preferable to keep plant pots off the floor, or they will need to be moved every time the flight is cleaned. Plant hangers are useful, being easily attached to an extra supporting beam of wood running down the centre of the roof unit.

Perennial plants with thickish stems which grow in, or can be trained into, a relatively horizontal position, such as *Aralia*, *Philodendron* and others, are ideal. These can be readily obtained from florists, and should be washed off carefully in case they are contaminated by any chemicals, before being placed in the flight. In addition, suitably-sized twigs can be positioned linking the sides with the front, taking care as always to ensure that the birds' tails will not be constantly rubbing on the netting when they use these perches.

2 Foodstuffs and their feeding

There is now a wide variety of foods prepared commercially for birds, ranging from the many brands of packeted seed to colour food, which as its name suggests, serves to maintain the plumage coloration of some species. A pet shop alone cannot supply all the bird's needs, however, as in most cases, the diet must also include a selection of fruit and greenfood given daily, as well as insects in some cases. The basic components of these foods are the same, being comprised of fat, carbohydrate and protein, as well as vitamins, minerals and water, but they may nevertheless vary quite widely, and so some variety should ensure a relatively balanced diet. Fruit such as grapes contain a relatively high proportion of water, and virtually no fat, whereas sunflower seed is a prime source of fats and is therefore a part of many seed mixtures.

The table below gives an indication of the relative proportions of the food components present in the main seeds fed to birds, although actual samples may differ somewhat, depending on various factors such as the growing conditions for a particular crop. They are grouped into two major categories; cereals, containing relatively high amounts of carbohydrate and low levels of fat, and oil seeds, for which the reverse is true.

Seed	Percentage of major food components		
	Carbohydrate	Protein	Fat
Millet	56	14	5
Canary seed	55	16	4
Oats	60	12	6
Maize	70	9	4
Rape	20	22	40
Hemp	25	16	30
Dutch Blue Maw	18	19	45
Linseed	23	23	34
Niger	22	21	40
Sunflower seed	20	24	47
Peanuts	19	26	47
Pine nuts	12	31	47

Various millets, as well as canary seed, are used in budgerigar seed mixtures, and although they differ in colour they are roughly circular. As a general rule, mixtures get cheaper as the proportion of millet increases. Some bird-keepers prefer to buy the seeds separately, and then produce their own blend. In the case of budgerigars, millets should never constitute more than 50 per cent of any mixture, and preferably nearer 20 per cent. Breeders feed relatively more canary seed when their birds are nesting, and indeed, for pet budgerigars, a diet of plain canary seed coupled with millet sprays given every other day is quite acceptable.

Millet sprays constitute the whole seedhead, and are eaten with relish by many species. Other types of millet, typically Pearl White and Dakota Red are, however, too hard for birds smaller than budgerigars. The diet of most finches is therefore based on panicum and Japanese millet, with a small amount of canary seed added, as well as some of the tonic seeds mentioned later.

Confusion can arise on occasions between canary seed itself, and seed fed to canaries, which is typically a mixture. The basic ingredients should be canary seed and red rape seed, in a ratio of three parts to one respectively, supplemented with other seeds, notably hemp. This is a relatively large brownish-black seed, contrasting with the colour of red rape and the ellipsoid yellowish appearance of canary seed. Being a source of the stimulant drug cannabis, hemp was a popular addition to canaries' diets during earlier centuries, as it was held to improve their vocal powers. The supply of hemp seed may be limited or restricted in some areas today because of its associated medical problems. It is sometimes sold in a crushed form, which is equally acceptable.

Hemp is usually the most popular seed in a canary mixture, but only relatively small amounts should be fed because it contains quite high levels of fat. Canaries are rather wasteful birds and do not hesitate to throw out the contents of their food pot all over the cage floor and elsewhere while looking for a particular seed, and if hemp proves a problem in this respect it must be fed separately.

Various seeds regarded as tonics by some breeders may nevertheless also be included in a standard seed mixture. These include niger, which is thin and black, and thought to have protective powers against egg-binding, being fed in larger amounts just before the breeding season. Linseed is offered prior to the moult, and should ensure the new plumage achieves a healthy gloss, but unfortunately many canaries refuse to take this flat, brown seed. Dutch Blue Maw is a very fine seed, obtained from poppies, which may be lost in a mixture and so is often sprinkled on top of soft food as described later. Gold-of-Pleasure, like the other seeds of this group, is often only available from larger pet stores or specialist bird seed suppliers. Perhaps surprisingly, by way of contrast, millet is very rarely fed to canaries, but in a communal flight cage they will often appreciate millet sprays. According to recent research, a canary's daily seed intake is approximately 5 grammes, when softfood is also offered.

Feeding parrot-type birds

Sunflower seed forms a major part of the diet of most members of the parrot family kept as pets. A budgerigar mixture, with an equal ration of sunflower is suitable for cockatiels, and some Australian Parrakeets, although this latter group are not suitable as pets. Conures and parrakeets from other continents should receive a parrot mixture, with a separate container of budgerigar seed. In addition, oats, or groats, which are simply dehusked oats, will be popular with some individuals, and a small quantity can be blended in with other seed.

Parrot mixtures vary somewhat in their ingredients but are comprised largely of sunflower seed. This annual plant produces seeds which may be black, white or striped, according to the variety concerned, of which the latter two types are most popular with bird-keepers. The size of seeds themselves also varies, especially in the case of the striped variety. Larger seeds generally produce a disproportionate amount of husk compared to kernel and so are more wasteful, as all psittacines remove the husk from the seed before consuming it.

Peanuts, also known as groundnuts because the pods themselves develop in the soil after being fertilized in the air, are an ingredient of most parrot mixtures. It is essential, particularly with peanuts, that they are free from any sign of mould, because contamination with *Aspergillus flavus* may have serious, if not fatal consequences. The aflatoxins produced by this mould are likely to produce both liver malfunction and cancer. Peanuts can be fed either loose or in their shells, but those packeted and prepared for human consumption should not be used because of their relatively high salt content, which may well prove harmful to a parrot.

Hemp seed is also included in parrot food, as is safflower, which is a small hard white seed, but rarely proves popular. Pieces of yellow, dried egg-biscuit meal are also found in some brands, and such foods offer a souce of animal protein to the birds. This is necessary because some of the individual amino acids present in protein that cannot be manufactured by the bird's liver must therefore be obtained from the diet. Those containing sulphur, such as lysine, are considered most important, and a deficiency may manifest itself in the form of poor quality feathering, and also perhaps odd patches of abnormal yellow plumage. This latter characteristic, seen especially in some Amazon Parrots, Ring-necked Parrakeets and *Pyrrhura* Conures is also likely to be related to stress, and the plumage may return to normal at the next moult.

Pine nuts have become widely used since 1975 in Britain although they must usually be purchased separately rather than as part of a mixture, and are not stocked by all seed suppliers. Indeed, the nuts are sometimes unobtainable, since they grow wild, being collected in the coniferous forests of China and Eastern Europe, with the former variety being somewhat smaller and paler in colour. It is well worth obtaining pine nuts, as they are very popular with all larger psittacines, down to conures and similar-sized parrakeets. They often prove particularly valuable for birds which otherwise would only eat sunflower seed, such as cockatoos.

While the commonly-available species should be offered such seeds as described above, the Galah or Roseate Cockatoo ought to be fed a diet relatively low in oil seeds. This is because these birds are susceptible to fatty tumours, known as lipomas, and their food intake may influence the development of such neoplasms. Although not malignant, they can prove a severe handicap to the bird, and may be too large to remove surgically, which is the only treatment available. Galah Cockatoos were widely kept in Europe, but are now much rarer, although they are popular pets in their homeland of Australia.

Apart from the cereals mentioned earlier, maize is a valuable food not only for these cockatoos but also for other larger parrots. It is extremely popular with dwarf macaws, who can crack this relatively hard seed, but for smaller species, it may be necessary to cook the required amount immersed in water, using a pressure cooker, until the maize is suitably softened. This or corn-on-the-cob is useful for all young parrots after weaning, as they may not necessarily take to a diet comprised exclusively of hard seed

Additional items for seed-eaters

A wide range of seeds can be soaked, which encourages their germination, and thus increases their protein levels. Millet sprays, submerged in a bowl of hot water for twenty-four hours then rinsed off thoroughly, are a very popular item when there are chicks in the nest. Oats, although fattening, can also be fed soaked, while black rape and teazle are prepared in this way for canaries.

In recent years, various beans available from health-food stores have become widely-used by breeders of parrots, and out of these, mung beans have attained the greatest popularity. Like other seeds, they can also be left to sprout after soaking, on damp blotting paper, and kept in a warm environment for a further couple of days. Providing there is no sign of mould on them, which is the major hazard, they can be fed directly to the birds, again after being rinsed.

Apart from such shoots, other greenfood, such as chickweed, is very popular with many species, ranging from small seed-eaters to large parrots. The use of herbicides and similar chemicals does mean that potential collecting sites may not be safe, however, and verges alongside roads are particularly dangerous from this viewpoint. Cultivated greens, such as perpetual spinach which grows easily from seed, are safer alternatives. Lettuce, if cut fresh, and fed in moderation, as with all greenfood, is safe, although some fanciers have reservations about its use.

Seeding grasses are welcomed by many species of finch, as well as budgerigars. It is possible to cultivate canary seed and even millet quite easily, although there is no guarantee that the crop will actually ripen successfully. Generally, supplies come from the warmer areas of the world, such as North Africa, especially Morocco, and Australia.

For the maximum chance of success, seed should be sown in late autumn, so that it has germinated by winter, growing rapidly in the following spring. Relatively poor soil is preferable, because otherwise leaf development takes precedence over that of the seedhead. If the crop does turn brown, the stems should be tied upside down in a dry environment, and just prior to feeding, the seedheads can be cut off. There is no need to extract the seed itself for most birds, but this can be achieved quite easily using a rolling pin.

The seedheads can also be used while still green, being appreciated by the birds in this form as well. For those without access to a garden, canary seed grows well in pots, and as an alternative, can be cut when about 5 cm (2 in) in height. It is also possible to purchase kits for growing similar grass in the home, but these are often expensive.

Fruit as described for softbills on pages 29–30 is appreciated by many parrots, and should also be offered daily, with an allowance of between a quarter and a half an apple per bird. Individuals do vary in their tastes, however, which can also be changeable. Some prefer peeled carrot to sweet apple for example. Powder tonics, containing vitamins and minerals, as well as the essential amino acids in a few cases, will adhere well to moist surfaces, and so are given to greatest effect on fruit rather than dry seed. There are also water-soluble preparations, which are administered in fluids. Many of these products have limited shelf-lives, and since only small amounts will be used, they should be obtained from stores with large turnovers, for maximum economy.

Calcium is a mineral which assumes major importance, along with phosphorus, in both growing and laying birds as it is a vital ingredient both of the skeletal system and egg-shell. All seedeaters should therefore have access to cuttlefish bone, obtained from a marine mollusc, which provides a large amount of calcium in a readily accessible form. The softer flaky surface of the bone is gnawed by the birds. However, in the case of canaries and finches particularly, their beaks may not be sufficiently powerful to gnaw off pieces, and small chunks, cut off with a knife, should therefore be available to them.

These bones can be purchased with seed from all pet stores, but are also occasionally found washed up on the beach. Providing they are not fouled in any way, they can be taken home and washed off thoroughly, before being soaked in water, which should be changed at least every day over the course of the next week. This should help to reduce their salt content. Subsequently, after being allowed to dry, they are suitable for feeding to the bird concerned. Softbills, whose diet is much less dependent on vegetable matter, which is notoriously low in calcium, are not given cuttlefish, but it will do no harm to powder some of the bone over their food occasionally.

Calcium within the body is under the control of Vitamin D_3, which is produced by the action of sunlight on the feathers and skin. Glass filters out the ultra-violet component responsible for the production of this vitamin, and so the bird's intake should be supplemented either via the diet or with artificial light. There are various natural lights now marketed largely for plants as well as reptiles, which contain this important component of sunlight, either in the form of tubes or bulbs of different wattages. The use of one of these lights in the room where the bird is living is therefore to be recommended for short periods each day. The vitamin is, however, stored in the liver, so deficiencies do not occur very suddenly.

The hard seeds eaten by birds must be broken down so they can be digested, and for this reason, grit must always be available to them. Smaller seedeaters including budgerigars consume relatively large amounts of grit, but larger parrots such as macaws rarely appear to sample it. Grit serves to grind up the food particles in the gizzard, which is a thick-walled muscular organ in seedeaters but much thinner in nectivores. A mixture of insoluble and soluble grit, with a little charcoal added is preferred, as this will also serve to meet part of the bird's mineral requirement, with the dissolving of some particles in the acid gizzard. Budgerigars are especially prone to goitre, which affects the thyroid glands in the neck, and so should be given oystershell grit, which is soluble, and an iodine block. Both of these measures will help to prevent a deficiency of this mineral occurring.

Softfood and colour feeding

Breeding canaries and finches usually receive a softfood, which is relatively high in protein, and packeted egg-biscuit mixtures are popular with most fanciers, although some still prepare such foods to their own traditional recipes. Wholemeal bread and milk, with water added in an equal volume is also valuable when the birds are rearing chicks.

Colour-feeding is rarely practised by pet bird owners, but is required for some species, especially some breeds of exhibition canary. Foreign birds, apart from psittacines, with red and related shades in their plumage are also fed a colouring agent to maintain this colour, which otherwise will fade significantly over the course of several moults.

The potential effect of colouring agents first became appreciated during the early years of the 1870s, when a moulting Norwich Fancy Canary was given cayenne pepper as a tonic. This resulted in a vast improvement in the bird's coloration, turning it to a rich shade of orange. Once the means of achieving such coloration became known, other natural colouring agents, including carrot juice, were discovered. Indeed, just feeding pieces of grated carrot on a regular basis to a moulting canary will have a noticeable effect on its coloration. At this time, the feathers are connected to the circulation, as shown by bleeding if an emerging feather is removed, whereas normal moulting of a feather is not accompanied by blood loss. Outside this period, there is likely to be no advantage in offering a colouring agent.

Colour-feeding is now, perhaps not surprisingly, more scientific with synthetic agents being used almost exclusively to give a natural, even effect in the plumage of birds ranging from flamingoes to canaries. If you plan to colour-feed a bird, take care to ensure that you add the correct amount to the water. The effects of an overdose last until the next moult, which will be approximately a year later, and show by giving the bird an abnormal, burnt appearance as well as reddish droppings. It should not actually cause any illness, however, because the chemical is virtually non-toxic. Ready-mixed colour foods, rather than a preparation for the water, are also produced.

The colour of this Scarlet Tanager (*Ramphocelus bresilius*) will soon fade if its diet is not supplemented with a suitable colouring agent.

Foods for softbills

There are various brands of softbill food now marketed, some of which can be fed direct from the packet, whereas others need moistening with water. Loose mixtures comprised of animal protein and honey, as well as vitamins and minerals are still most widely used in Europe, but pelleted forms, once confined to America, are now becoming more widely available elsewhere. Smaller granules are also available, depending on the size of the bird. It is probably preferable to soak both pellets and granules in water for about fifteen minutes prior to feeding, which allows them to expand to approximately twice their original size in some cases, without breaking up. After straining off the water, they can be fed on their own, or mixed in with fruit as is loose softbill food.

Mynah birds, which are the most commonly kept pet softbills, take readily to such pellets without any difficulties as a general rule, even if they previously have been fed on loose brands. Changes to the diet of all softbills should be carried out over a week or so, however, rather than suddenly, to minimize the risk of subsequent digestive disturbances.

Toucans and related species which cannot feed on loose softbill food, unless it is mixed well and thus adheres to solid chunks of fruit, must be offered pellets. As a general rule, the birds will select the fruit first, and leave the majority of such pellets until last. It is important, if they are to receive a balanced diet, that the pellets are consumed, and so only the required amount of food for the bird concerned should be given daily. This will soon be obvious from experience, and initially, two smaller feeds can be offered each day, to ensure the pellets are eaten. In the case of seed-eating birds, though, there is no need to ration them in this way, partly because their dry seed is not a perishable foodstuff.

Sweet apples form the basis of the fruit ration for many softbills, whether kept as pets or in flights, and one or two per day should be allowed for a Hill Mynah. All fruit should be washed thoroughly and peeled as necessary, with apples being quartered and diced into cubes approximately 1.25 cm (0.5 in) in size. Unlike parrots, mynah birds cannot gnaw off chunks effectively from a whole apple, and if the diced pieces are too large, preventing the bird from swallowing them whole, they will be wasted. The small narrow-billed softbills such as Sugar Birds will suffer the same difficulty unless they are presented with suitably-sized pieces, whereas stout-beaked species such as tanagers are quite able to nibble off mouthfuls from larger chunks.

Seedless grapes are ideal for mynahs since they can usually be swallowed whole, and invariably prove popular. As with all fruit offered to birds, only firm grapes should be selected. Larger grapes do not necessarily have to be stoned, as these will be passed through the birds' digestive tract, along with the skin of the fruit, without harm, but they may need to be cut up as they are often too big. A quantity purchased in season can always be stored successfully in a freezer, and providing the grapes are spread out individually during the freezing process so that they remain separate, any number can be removed

Pelleted diets are now produced for mynahs and other softbills. The Hill Mynah (*Gracula religiosa*) shown here is the most talented talker of the group as a whole.

with ease at a later date. A clean disused ice-cream container makes an ideal receptacle for such fruit in the freezer.

Raisins or sultanas soaked overnight, and then washed off thoroughly also offer useful variety to the diet if fed at intervals. Dried fruit, however, contains more carbohydrate than its fresh equivalent, and so can prove somewhat fattening, particularly if the bird does not have much exercise.

Amongst other fruits, there are some which are viewed with caution by bird-keepers. Bananas, which are sticky by nature and therefore messy to feed, are ripened by mechanical means in most cases and this is said to lead to digestive upsets, particularly in the smaller species. Orange is not popular with most birds because of its acid nature, but tomatoes, which also contain high levels of Vitamin C, are taken readily by many mynahs and toucans, and so can be offered in moderation as a supplement to the basic diet.

Insect food

The softbills covered in this book are all omnivores, rather than frugivores dependent solely on fruit to meet their body's requirements. Indeed, it is extremely doubtful if any species is able to survive on a diet of fruit alone, and certainly the vast majority take some insects, or small reptiles and mammals, and even other chicks, to supply the food elements lacking in fruit. This requirement must be fulfilled in the diets of birds living in an artificial environment.

Mealworms are the most popular means of supplying live-food, because they are clean and easy to keep, with no noxious problems, unlike fly larvae, which can prove lethal unless treated in the correct manner prior to feeding. Like other insects, mealworms go through a life cycle beginning when the egg hatches, giving rise to the larva, which matures through successive moults before pupating and finally emerging as an adult meal-beetle. The mealworms themselves are the larval form, although subsequent stages can also be used as bird food.

A suitable closed receptacle, with air holes in its lid, half-filled with bran should be prepared to store the mealworms after purchase. The addition of a powder tonic to the bran is useful to improve their subsequent feeding value. Pieces of apple should be placed on top of the bran to provide moisture, but it must not actually be moistened because moulds are then likely to develop in the container itself. When kept under such conditions, the mealworms will thrive, and storing them in a relatively cool environment between $5 - 10°C$ ($40 - 50°F$) will slow their metabolism and thus prevent them from changing into beetles too fast. The complete life cycle will take about four months when these insects are kept in a temperature of 25°C (76.5°F).

Mealworms must only be fed to the birds in moderation, with a daily ration of up to ten being suitable for a mynah bird. They are not, however, ideal for Sugar Birds and similar-sized softbills, partly because of their hard outer covering of chitin, which is relatively indigestible. Moulting mealworms, instantly recognizable by their white, soft cuticle are relatively safe, however, providing only a couple are given each day. At this stage, they are also useful for breeding waxbills, which become largely insectivorous during this period. In an emergency, you can scald the mealworms, remove as much of the softened exoskeleton as possible, and offer them to small birds.

The ideal livefood for small nectivores is fruit flies (*Drosophilia*), and the mutant form lacking wings is infinitely preferable for birds kept indoors as it cannot escape into the room. Old banana skins placed outside in jam-jars serve to attract these minute flies, which can then be fed on a sugar mixture *in situ*, and they should soon start breeding in a warm environment. A muslin cover over the top of the jar will restrain them, and then a small square cut out of it enables the flies to escape into the cage without the bird itself getting stuck in the jar. Some aquarist shops also stock these flies.

Aphids are another popular source of livefood both for nectivores and finches like waxbills. Stems or leaves with aphid colonies can be collected from a garden where no insecticides are used, and either fed directly or transferred to a narrow-necked vessel containing water. They can then be consumed by the birds over a longer period, as the plant material remains fresh.

Nectar mixtures

It is now possible to purchase nectar pastes and powders, which are diluted with water, but many aviculturists make up their own recipes. Preparation of nectar mixtures is not complicated, but needs to be carried out daily, although a surplus can be kept from the morning in a refrigerator and then given in the evening, after being allowed to warm up for a quarter of an hour beforehand. The solution should not be either excessively hot or cold, but just tepid to the touch. Under no circumstances should fresh nectar be added to an old solution, because severe digestive upsets and even fatalities are likely to result, with bacteria and other harmful micro-organisms developing on this sugar medium. All vessels must also be kept immaculately clean for the same reason.

Elderberries are popular with Tanagers like this Golden Tanager (*Tangara arthus goodsoni*).

Below Mealworm larvae are widely-used as livefood for many softbills such as this Green Honeycreeper (*Chlorophanes spiza*).

The mixture will vary somewhat according to the species concerned, a typical solution for lories being made by dissolving one dessertspoonful of glucose powder, with a half of malt using a small amount of boiling water in the first instance. Having made the volume up to 500cc with cold water, add a quarter of a dessertspoon of condensed milk, and half of a proprietary baby cereal food like 'Farex', along with a few drops of a vitamin preparation such as 'Abidec' (Parke-Davis). This is useful for all birds, providing a valuable source of Vitamin A, which is likely to be deficient in seed, as well as Vitamin D and various other components. The suggested dose for a budgerigar is 0.3ml, given in the water twice weekly. Excessive overdosage is likely to prove harmful, however, as some of these chemicals will accumulate in the liver.

A different mixture for small nectivores, such as Sugar Birds, is made up with one teaspoonful of honey plus one eggspoonful of 'Complan' dissolved as before, in a total volume of 150cc. A second drinker, comprised just of honey water without any Complan is also desirable, so the birds can regulate their intake. The honey provides a source of sugars for energy, while the other ingredient contains protein, an excess of which may lead to gout, manifested by swellings of the digits. Drinking water must also always be available to nectar-feeding species, as in the case of all birds. Never offer nectar mixtures in open pots however, in case the birds try to bathe in them, as this will have catastrophic results.

3 Daily care

Dealing with a new arrival

Birds will take a varying length of time to settle in an unfamiliar environment, with smaller species generally adapting more quickly than larger individuals. Parrots, especially, may remain shy for a week or longer. A daily routine should be adopted from the outset, and this in itself, if carried out slowly and sensibly with no sudden movements, will help to reassure a nervous bird.

The cage should have been washed out thoroughly, and made ready in advance of the bird's arrival, with full food and water pots already in place. Most birds will move quite readily into the light, and so to save unnecessary handling, carefully undo one of the box flaps and place the opening over the cage door. A gentle tap on the back or sides of the box should then encourage the bird out, after which it must be left quiet, and given adequate opportunity to feed before being covered for the night.

The cover should fit roughly over the whole cage, allowing adequate air space for ventilation. Parrots in strange surroundings often prefer to hold the bars of the cage, rather than using the perch, so it is important that the material of the cover is not likely to snag a claw. When frightened, parrots will grip tightly with their whole foot, and so if the cover is suddenly removed, severe injury may result from a claw being caught up. Indeed, lifting the cover vertically is preferable to just pulling it off, as there is less risk of the bird taking flight wildly.

Problems are most likely to occur with a new arrival, and so a close watch should be kept on its eating habits, droppings and general demeanour over the first crucial weeks. A variation in the colour of the droppings need not be indicative of disease, however, as this can be influenced by the bird's food. Softbills fed various fruits may have different droppings, according to the fruit concerned, while in budgerigars, feeding coloured seed treats can have the same effect.

The position of the cage in the home is also significant in helping the bird to settle in satisfactorily. It must be located out of draughts and at a reasonable height, from where it can see around most of the room. Fumes can be very detrimental to a bird's health, and for this reason and that of hygiene, they should never be kept in a kitchen. Some fatalities are thought to have resulted from the fumes given off by non-stick cooking pots which have over-heated. Open fires can also be dangerous.

A well-lit location is preferable, but the bird must never be exposed to the direct rays of the sun. Although many species do hail from tropical countries, they always have the opportunity to seek shade. Once the temperature rises to about 32°C (90°F), signs of heat stress, shown by gasping and the positioning of the wings away from the body, become manifest. A slight tremor may also be noticed. Prolonged exposure to a temperature much above 40°C (105°F) will rapidly prove fatal.

Introducing a companion

The introduction of a companion for an established bird will require careful monitoring, and must always be planned for a time when someone will be present in the same room. It is sensible to keep the birds apart for at least a week, so that the new arrival can settle down satisfactorily. If, by any chance, it does fall ill, then the likelihood of an infection spreading to its proposed mate is also reduced, particularly if it is always attended to last.

There is always a danger that the new bird will be bullied by the other at first, and so under no circumstances should it be placed directly into the cage or flight of its partner. This will be viewed as a distinct intrusion of an established territory, and separating two fighting macaws, for example, does not prove a very easy or pleasant task. Indeed, many parrots that have formed human attachments can become very spiteful towards others of their kind, which are viewed as rivals for their owner's attention. Even other pets, such as dogs, may be seen in this light, provoking an outburst of uncontrolled screeching. Such behaviour can also occur in smaller species, including *Brotogeris* parrakeets and many conures.

As a first step, therefore, in getting the birds acquainted, they should be confined to cages relatively near to each other, but never so close together that they could bite the other bird's feet. In the case of a flight cage divided into two parts for this purpose, severe injuries of this type may result unless the division is either solid or comprised of a double partition, wired on opposite sides of a 5 cm (2 in) square frame. The mesh should be of a suitable diameter to prevent the species concerned from sticking its head through, and in all cases, 2.5 × 1.25 cm (1 × $\frac{1}{2}$ in) is quite satisfactory.

Finches are much less quarrelsome, however, but it is still sensible to introduce them on neutral ground, confining them both in a cage before releasing them into a flight for example. Different species intended to live alongside existing birds in a flight may be accepted without difficulty, such as the inclusion of small Chinese Painted Quail, which spend much of their time on the floor anyway.

Fighting is always more likely to occur when the birds start nesting. Then pairs that have lived together quite happily may suddenly become aggressive towards their companions. It is important not to overstock a small flight, but be content to have perhaps only a single pair of birds housed there. The chances of successful breeding are then much increased, and the enjoyment of watching the family develop is not likely to be marred by tragic outbreaks of squabbling. Even a minor dispute may cause a breeding pair to desert their nest and its contents.

Feeding management and suitable containers

Seed should only be purchased from reputable suppliers, and generally the packeted brands vary less in their quality than loose samples. These must always appear clean, and free from debris, such as stones. Dust is also potentially harmful, and seed showing any signs of mouse dirt, damp or moulds should never even be considered.

The feeding value of seed declines gradually but progressively following harvesting. Oil seeds can be safely stored for two and a half years, before feeding while cereals such as canary seed may be kept for a maximum of five years. It is, however, preferable to buy relatively small quantities, which should help to ensure that the seed is as fresh as possible.

Seed is likely to sweat when kept in closed plastic containers unless there is adequate air-flow, especially in a warm environment. This must be avoided, because once damp, the seed will begin to sprout, and moulds may also develop, so the whole quantity will have to be discarded. Ventilation holes punched in the top of a disused large ice-cream container, or a clean screw-top jar serve to overcome this problem.

A food container which clips over the cage bars

A very wide range of feeding vessels is now available, and most cages come complete with such utensils. Some of the plastic-based models described earlier have hooded containers at either end of the cage, which close over when the pot itself is removed, thus preventing the bird escaping. In the case of young birds, however, they may not be used to this means of feeding and thus starve themselves as a result. Some seed sprinkled at first around the base of the pot will serve to attract their attention, and they soon learn to adapt accordingly. If given a free choice between this and an open pot, most birds will opt for the latter container. Faced with a hood, instinct suggests that it could be dangerous, as they cannot see their surroundings, and thus possible predators, when feeding and at their most vulnerable.

Drinkers

The other pot in budgerigar-type cages is usually used for grit, with water being provided in a separate closed container clipping on to the wire of the cage. The clips supplied in most cages are adjustable, fitting between either horizontal or vertical bars. In the former case, however, the bars themselves may need to be bent slightly to accommodate the drinker itself. Such plastic drinkers can also be used on flights being located at a convenient height above a perch, and will also dispense sugar and nectar mixtures. It is preferable to buy the largest size available, because especially when breeding, or during periods of hot weather, the birds will require more fluid.

Parrots will often chew the ends of such drinkers, so the closed bottles with metal spouts, relying on a gravity-flow system for delivery, are useful for these birds. Unfortunately parrots soon learn to detach such bottles if the hook is not reinforced, and these may then break, spilling water all over the floor and depriving the bird itself of the fluid.

A closed water container

Bathing

The major advantages of drinkers over open pots of water is that the birds have an uncontaminated supply and are not able to soak surrounding furniture by bathing. A regular daily spray for parrots, with tepid water to which a plumage conditioner can be added, must however be viewed as essential, if they are deprived of access to an open bath, or choose to ignore it. The water helps to damp down their feather dust, which otherwise is scattered around the room, and also serves to stimulate natural water-proofing of the plumage, thus improving its appearance. Special budgerigar baths to fit on the cage door, and enclosed on three sides to prevent water being scattered everywhere, are available as an alternative for smaller birds.

Softbills also appreciate bathing, and most mynah birds delight in being sprayed. The sprays sold for plants, giving out a very fine jet of water, are ideal for the purpose, and, in the case of a planted flight, also serve their original purpose of improving the condition of the vegetation. The leaves of some plants become very soiled with droppings, and these may need to be replaced on occasions and cleaned off accordingly.

Additional vessels

Open plastic pots, which hook over the mesh at the sides of the cage or the flight prove useful, as additions to the vessels included as part of a cage. Such additional containers can be used to provide softfood, and make a suitable receptacle for mealworms, to prevent them escaping before they are eaten. Galvanized metal pots are to be preferred for the larger parrots, but should not be used as water containers, when a tonic is being used. The surface of the metal may react unfavourably with the added chemicals in the water, and this also applies in the case of antibiotic treatments administered by this route.

Both metal and plastic bases, designed to fit a jam-jar acting as a seed reservoir are also produced. These are very useful for delivering the small cereal seeds, such as canary and millet, but the majority will become blocked by sunflower seed. They are ideal for a flight cage containing budgerigars or finches, and ensure that there is a constant supply of seed available, which will not require topping up daily. In addition, the seed is again unlikely to be contaminated by the birds' droppings.

Wire racks to hold greenfood are also produced, but do not really prove very satisfactory, simply because the bird will still pull pieces on to the floor of its cage. Cuttlefish clips are useful to hold pieces of this bone, without having to wedge it through the cage bars.

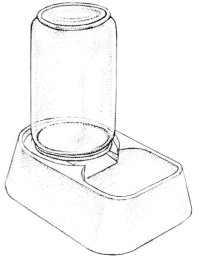

A jam-jar seed reservoir with a plastic base

Toys

Swings are included in most cages, but are only appreciated by a proportion of birds. If a swing is ignored, then it should be removed, and substituted with a natural perch. Birds generally prefer to use firm perches, so it is not surprising that some feel distinctly uneasy when confronted with a swing.

Plastic toys of all types can be seen on the shelves of pet stores, and although they may appear attractive, too many will simply serve to clutter the cage, making the bird's life miserable. A simple mirror which clips on to the cage bars is probably quite adequate, along with a ping-pong ball, which will be light enough for the bird to roll about the floor, if it so wishes. Ladders are also available, but these take up a lot of space in a standard budgerigar-type cage.

Simple toys are often most suitable and easy to clean, and for parrots, a wooden cotton-reel with the labels removed can provide hours of fascination. It can either be threaded through the cage bars, or left loose on the floor. The commercially-available items designed primarily for budgerigars are not suitable for parrots as they will be destroyed. Thin wire only

A wide range of toys are produced for budgerigars.

should be used to hang such toys, never wool or similar material which could be accidentally ingested by the bird, perhaps with fatal consequences. Parrots are often interested in a mirror positioned so they can see their reflection, but out of reach of their beaks. Birds also seem to find the noise of a transistor radio appealing, perhaps regarding it as some form of company when no-one is in the same room. Song birds are also often encouraged to give voice when they are played music.

Cleaning the bird's environment

Regular cleaning of the cage and its utensils will be required to keep the bird in good health. This applies especially in the case of softbills, with their copious droppings, and mynahs for example, will need to be cleaned out at least daily. Seed-eaters generally ought to have their cages re-lined about every other day. The perches must also be washed off at frequent intervals, and while those in cages housing nectivores may appear quite clean, they are often sticky because of the bird's diet. Indeed, if dirt is allowed to accumulate on the cage floor, the perches themselves in turn will become heavily soiled, with the bird transferring muck on its feet. When this happens, droppings picked up from the floor may also harden around a toe, cutting off the blood circulation in the process. The digit will then eventually be lost, unless rapid action is taken to remove the debris by careful soaking.

The covering used on the floor of the flight or cage varies, partly according to the species concerned. Budgerigars and canaries are traditionally kept with sandsheets at the bottom of the cage. These are produced in different sizes, which should correspond to the sand tray of the cage concerned. While such sheets are quite adequate to collect their droppings, some hen budgerigars especially, will often cause a mess by shredding them up. Such behaviour is usually sporadic, and can often be linked to the breeding season. Most parrot-like birds become more destructive at this time. As an alternative to sandsheets, loose bird sand can be used, but may prove somewhat abrasive, if it becomes stuck to any part of the body. Sand is also messier than the sheets, and can be scattered outside the cage, along with the seed husks themselves.

In the case of softbills, a more absorbent material is to be recommended, and a sheaf of old newspapers makes an economic and functional covering for the cage floor. Paper towelling is a more aesthetic alternative which can be considered, and either covering in fact can be used for any bird. Colour sheets should be avoided in the case of species which may chew up their floor covering, as they could contain harmful inks. When using paper, it is useful either to fold it over, or use an adhesive tape to attach it roughly outside the cage, because paper lacks the rigidity of a sandsheet. As a result, when the bird flies to another perch, the paper may well be disturbed by the draught, with the result that the droppings accumulate directly on the cage floor, rather than on the intended covering. This makes cleaning more difficult.

Outside the bird's own environment, there is always the problem of seed husks and other debris spreading to nearby furniture, and down on to the floor. During periods of moulting, the number of loose feathers will also increase dramatically. It is possible to purchase plastic covers to fit round the base of some cages, which help to reduce the amount of dirt spread into the room itself, while clear perspex screens can also be made, for the same purpose.

The most satisfactory means of cleaning up such debris is to use a vacuum cleaner which has an additional sucking attachment. Sunflower seed husks are rather solid to be picked up satisfactorily using a straightforward cleaner, larger feathers are almost impossible to pick up. Such an attachment can be further employed around the cage or flight itself, to remove debris from corners and other similar sites before it spreads outside. Dust raised by brushing the floor of the flight or the room is also kept to a minimum by this means. When birds are still in a flight being cleaned using an attachment, the machine itself should be situated as far as possible away from it, so that the noise level is kept to the minimum.

Furniture close at hand will also need to be dusted quite frequently, but aerosol polishes should be used with the utmost caution in a room where birds are kept. Some people claim to have lost their pets as a result of using these sprays. Metal polish must never be applied to cage bars.

Allowing a bird liberty in a room

This, as suggested previously, is not always desirable from either the owner's or bird's viewpoints, unless the latter is very tame and thus easily caught. Liberty in a room does give a bird kept in a cage a means of achieving regular flying exercise, however. Valuable ornaments will need to be removed beforehand, in case they are knocked over by the bird.

There are several elementary precautions which must be taken prior to letting a bird out of its cage, and someone should always then be present in order to intervene if the need arises. All windows must be securely closed and fitted with net curtains, to indicate to the bird that there is an obstacle

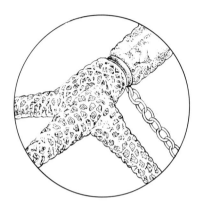

Leg chains are potentially very dangerous, and should never be used

present. Other possible hazards, such as fireplaces, also need to be covered, not forgetting any cat-flaps that might be cut into the door of the room. It may seem very obvious, but the location of the cat itself should always be reliably ascertained, prior to opening the cage door. Hoods must be fitted to aquarium tanks, while plants which may be poisonous if consumed by the bird, such as ivy or *Dieffenbachia* (Dumb Cane) will have to be removed from the room. Other potential dangers, especially in older properties, are peeling paintwork and crumbling plasterwork, as these are likely to contain lead, which is very toxic.

Parrots out of their cages are often trained to sit on a T-shaped stand, with food and water pots at either end, in addition to a tray at the base, which catches their droppings and spilt seed. While such stands are useful, the barbaric practice of attaching the bird to the perch using a leg chain should never be adopted. If it is desired to restrain a parrot from flying in the room (which surely is the main purpose of letting it out) then the flight feathers of one wing only should be cut across cleanly.

Clipping a wing, although an unnecessary mutilation, is infinitely preferable to the serious injuries likely to result when a bird which is attached to a leg chain suddenly takes flight. The procedure should never be carried out while the bird is moulting, because severe bleeding is likely since the feathers are still receiving a blood supply. They need to be cut quite short, although not down to the base of the quills. A clean cut right across the whole wing will not subsequently appear as disfiguring as cutting individual feathers in turn. If in any doubt whatsoever about the procedure, then the bird should be taken to a vet. Indeed, clipping the wing may result in the bird losing confidence in its owner for a short while if he carries out the task himself. It will need to be repeated about each moult, otherwise the effects of the handicap will be lost as new feathers emerge.

Before being let out of its cage, the bird should be quite tame, and ready to sit on the hand. It is possible to position a number of perches, suitable to take a budgerigar's weight, around a room, using removable sucker pads to attach them to the walls, or a mirror. The cage door should always be left open, so that, the bird can return of its own accord to feed. Parrots are often quite content merely to climb out and sit on top of the cage, returning when a suitable tit-bit is placed inside. This does not always happen, however, especially at first, and then the bird will need to be caught. Conversely, some parrots are shy when their cage door is first opened, and prove reluctant to leave, but given time they will pluck up the

Holding a bird, here seen from the side

courage to emerge, and they will soon be enjoying their new-found freedom.

Catching a loose bird in a room

Finches are without doubt the hardest birds to catch in a room, because they are so quick on the wing. Since they also prove generally reluctant to return to the cage independently, these birds are rarely let out.

When faced with catching a loose bird, without a padded net to hand, the best solution is to darken the room as much as possible, by drawing any available curtains. Most birds will stay in one location when darkness descends so, barring any obstacles that might be in the way, it should be possible to creep up quietly and catch the bird using cupped hands.

If this proves impossible, there is little point in chasing it wildly around the room. The bird will soon become stressed, breathing heavily, perhaps with its mouth open, and is likely to die if pursued relentlessly for a long period. On no account should a parrot-like bird be let out of its cage without a suitable pair of gloves in the same room, so that, if necessary, it can be caught safely. A stout pair of gauntlets is recommended for handling Amazons and similar-sized birds, although they serve to reduce the wearer's sensitivity. Towels rather than gloves are sometimes suggested, but must be considered more dangerous for both parties. The bird's claws will rapidly become entangled in the material, which will offer the handler much less protection than gloves. A bite from a cockatoo or large parrot can cause a severe injury, while even budgerigars may give a painful nip.

Many people unused to catching birds are rightly afraid of hurting them, but at the same time attempt to grab them tightly to restrain them. It is much better to make this a two-stage process; once having caught the bird, attention can be given to restraining it safely yet securely. A finch, for example, struggling between the palms of the hands will not in fact be injured, unless it is held too tightly. The bird can then be transferred to the palm of one hand only, which is usually the left in the case of a right-handed person, with its head emerging in the circle created by the thumb and first finger.

With species that bite, a slightly different position will be required, to keep the beak away from the fingers. It is common to restrain a budgerigar, for example, with its head gently held between the first and second fingers of the appropriate hand. In this position, most birds will stop struggling, and can be examined relatively easily. It is also possible to administer treatments such as a scaly-face lotion, or cut the beak without

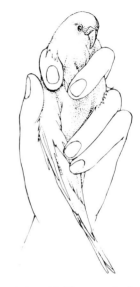

Restraining a bird between the first two fingers. If the bird's head is twisted to the side, it can peck the fingers holding it

A view of the correct position, with a toucanet firmly restrained

Leg chains, as shown here attached to a Red and Gold Macaw (*Ara macao*) should never be used for such birds.

fear of the bird moving its head suddenly. Handling should always be kept to a minimum as it is stressful. Canaries, in particular, have a reputation for fainting if held too tightly, but placed back in their cage, they will generally recover if there is no other underlying reason for such behaviour.

Problems out-of-doors

Birds can be moved outside for short periods on warm days, providing there is someone in their vicinity to protect them against cats, and that they have adequate protection from direct sunlight and wind. The door of the cage must be doubly secured as an additional precaution.

There are, unfortunately, occasions when in spite of all precautions a bird will escape, either outside or from a room, leaving a heart-broken owner behind. Such a loss should be reported at once to a local radio station, as many will help to track down lost pets, while details inserted in local shop windows and neighbourhood newspapers may prove fruitful. You can also contact an official of the nearest bird club, in case one of the members either catches or is brought the escapee.

After locating the bird, it may take a lot of patience before it can be caught successfully. The cage should be put in a fairly open position, with its door being held open by a long piece of taut string running to a concealed observer. A millet spray or seed located prominently in the cage should serve to attract the bird down, and encourage it to enter its cage. If the string is attached to a door which closes with a spring, it can immedi-

Far right This Superb Tanager (*Tangara fastuosa*) is moulting, and so its plumage appears tatty, but it is otherwise alert.

New feathers emerge wrapped in sheaths, as shown here on the head and tail

ately be allowed to slacken, and the door should swing swiftly shut, catching the bird inside. This might not even be necessary in the case of a very tame individual, which may choose to fly down and land on its owner's shoulder, especially when tempted by a tit-bit.

Moulting

By providing the bird with a varied, balanced diet throughout the year however, you are less likely to encounter problems during the moulting period. It is important to bear in mind that a diet for parrots based entirely on sunflower seed, for example, will be low in Vitamin A, which helps to protect the body against infections.

If possible, such birds should be encouraged to eat pellets, in addition to seed, simply because these are specially formulated and offer a more varied diet. Then when the bird starts to moult, it will be in a better physical condition, which should help it through this debilitating period.

4 Breeding and colour inheritance

The species most likely to breed successfully in the home are considered in detail later, whereas this chapter is primarily concerned with means of encouraging them to nest successfully. Psittacines as a general rule cannot be expected to raise chicks in the domestic environment, with the notable exception of the budgerigar, but occasional successes have been reported for various species.

One of the most notable was the first British breeding of an Orange-winged Amazon Parrot. The hen, Sylvie, thought to be about twelve years old, had been kept by Mr and Mrs Davis for six years before she nested. The cock, obtained three years previously when Sylvie first started showing signs of nesting activity, was later to be responsible for taking over the rearing duties as their chick grew older. Such behaviour is quite natural in many species, and would appear to enable the hen to lay again, unmolested by the demands of her previous chicks.

A single youngster was hatched by Sylvie, in a nestbox located on top of the cupboard used to house the children's toys. Although the birds' temperament did not alter in this case, some individuals can become aggressive when breeding. Tame parrots are especially dangerous then, because they often have no natural fear of humans, and can inflict severe bites on the unsuspecting. The temperament of even single birds housed on their own may also suddenly change in this way for the same reason.

Apart from the budgerigar, lovebirds and cockatiels are most likely to nest in the home, but require large flight cages and nestboxes compared to the smaller breeding cages used for budgerigars. There is always a possibility, however, that given sufficient privacy and care, other parrot-like birds will breed successfully while in a domestic environment. In some cases it might be difficult to obtain true pairs in the first instance, as the species concerned may not be sexually dimorphic, so there is no characteristic plumage difference separating the sexes.

In such instances, when selecting a companion, cocks can sometimes be recognized because they are often bigger than

A crested Grey Zebra Finch (*Taeniopygia guttata*) cock.

Below A hollow log adapted to form a nestbox.

hens, with larger beaks, but this is no absolute guarantee. Various methods of clinical sexing are now becoming available to serious breeders of such birds, with surgical (endoscopic) and DNA examinations being most commonly used today. In the former case, the reproductive organs are viewed by a veterinarian using a special instrument called an endoscope. This is inserted via a small incision made through the body wall. DNA sexing is carried out in a laboratory, and the bird does not need to be anaesthetised for this purpose, which makes it safer than surgical sexing. Instead, a blood sample is taken from the bird, and the DNA is extracted, enabling its gender to be determined.

It is possible to sex some birds when they come into breeding condition, and this applies not only in the case of canaries, but also Bengalese Finches. Both these and Zebra Finches will usually breed satisfactorily in the home, and may prove quite prolific. Cock Bengalese start singing persistently to their intended mates, and fan their tails out during their display, so they can be clearly recognized. In the case of such birds, obtaining several at the outset should ensure that at least one potential pair will be present. Bengalese, unlike some other species, are also quite amenable together when housed in small groups.

Mutations are seen in the most free-breeding species, simply because there is thus a greater chance of a mutant colour gene arising in a particular strain, as more chicks are bred. The appearance of such genes occurs randomly with a proportion proving lethal, and this can apply in the case of all crested varieties, as explained later. Individuals of any colour can be paired safely together, but it may be thought preferable to select for a certain colour or characteristic in the adults, in the hope that this will be passed on to the next generation. Such considerations figure prominently in the minds of exhibition breeders, who usually maintain detailed pedigree records of their studs and put great thought into their pairings.

Breeding accommodation

Box-type breeding cages, as distinct from the wire cages used for pet birds, are widely used for budgerigars, canaries and certain finches, especially Zebras and Bengalese. Such cages can be constructed quite easily, preferably from plywood, using the appropriate front for the species concerned, or may be purchased ready for use. Once again, the biggest cage available is likely to yield the most satisfactory results, giving the birds adequate space for exercise. Particular attention must be given to the perches, because if these are loose, then satisfactory mating may not occur. These cages traditionally have a

A variety of nesting sites will be used by birds. Nesting baskets are often preferred by finches, open nests by canaries and nestboxes by budgerigars.

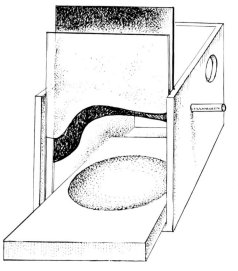

A budgerigar nestbox

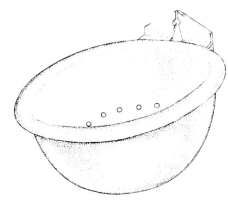

A canary nestpan

light emulsion interior, and can also be painted on the outside if desired.

Budgerigars require a nestbox, which fits most conveniently on to the outside of the cage at one end, with a corresponding hole cut through the side of the cage to give the birds access. In this position, it is much easier to inspect the nest than if the box is located inside the cage itself. Finches will also breed in a similar set-up of this type, although of course they require a smaller nestbox. These can be purchased separately, as with budgerigar nestboxes, if required. There is also a variety of small wicker baskets and barrels for finches which hook over a suitable part of the cage or flight. The nesting receptacle should always be placed high up pointing away from direct light, to give the birds an increased sense of security. Bright light shining through an entrance may deter the birds from using the box.

Canaries differ somewhat in their requirements, and breed in open pans rather than boxes. These are screwed on to the back of the cage, with plastic designs now being most popular. An encircling nesting felt, acting as a liner should be stitched in at the base of the pan. The birds then build their own nest on top of the liner, using specially prepared material or hamster bedding, both of which are sold by most pet stores. Hay is not recommended for nesting material, because it may be contaminated with spores of the fungus *Aspergillus fumigatus*. Under the moist and warm conditions prevailing when there are chicks in the nest, such spores may develop, affecting the birds. Aspergillosis is a serious disease, which affects the airways and lungs, and currently cannot be cured, although tests using a preventative vaccine are currently being carried out in America.

Finches should also be offered nesting material, but especially in the case of Zebras, additional supplies ought to be withheld once the hen has laid, because they tend to carry on building, even on top of their eggs. Budgerigars only require a plain wooden base with a concavity, thus known as a concave, for the hen to lay her eggs in, and then rear the chicks. Such concaves require changing at regular intervals once the chicks are growing well. There are two genera of psittacines, lovebirds and hanging parrots, that use nesting material on a regular basis, and they should be given thin branches complete with leaves.

Breeding behaviour

A change in behaviour is usually noted immediately prior to breeding, as suggested previously. Hen canaries and other finches begin searching the floor of their cage for possible nesting material, carrying it around in their beaks. Cocks become more vocal, taking an increased interest in their intended mates. In budgerigars, the cere of the hen turns deep brown, and she becomes more destructive, quite frequently reducing a cuttlefish bone to virtual powder over the course of a day or so. Cocks in turn sing for longer periods, while constricting the pupils of their eyes, as is commonly seen in other psittacines, and banging their beaks on a perch. Direct courtship involves the cock making vertical head movements in front of the hen, before feeling her and finally mating. A whole clutch can be fertilized following a single successful mating.

The droppings of most species change somewhat in character when the hen is laying. They become much larger in the case of budgerigars, whereas many hen parrots pass brownish rather than green motions which have a strong odour. This is not a cause for concern, providing that the bird otherwise appears well. Incubation is often carried out by the hen alone, or her mate may assist, depending on the species concerned. Cocks share this duty in the case of the cockatiel and most cockatoos, whereas female canaries bear the burden of hatching the eggs alone. From this stage onwards, the birds should not be disturbed more than necessary.

Budgerigars lay their eggs every other day, whereas finches produce a clutch without these daily gaps. Canary breeders frequently remove the eggs from the hen as they are laid, substituting dummy replacements obtained from a pet store, until the fourth egg has been produced. All the eggs are then returned and this should ensure that the chicks in turn hatch close together, and, being of similar size, are thus more likely to survive as a group. The incubation period varies, depending on the species concerned.

Once the chicks have hatched, the food requirements of their parents will be increased, and so additional supplies, previously offered in small quantities from the first signs of breeding activity, must now be available. The rearing foods sold by many pet stores for canaries are also useful for finches, and should be given in separate open containers, located either on the floor or hooked to the wire near a perch. Wholemeal bread is another alternative food, when softened with equal parts of milk and water, and can also be sprinkled with a powder tonic. Such foods are perishable, and so should be taken out each evening after the birds have fed. This also applies to fruit and greenfood, which wilts quite rapidly indoors.

The pots themselves must be washed out thoroughly, initially with a detergent to remove food particles and traces of grease, before being rinsed off, ready for further use. It is possible to prepare simple disposable containers for canaries and finches, such as clean yoghurt pots cut down to a suitable size, which are then discarded after a single feed.

Breeding disappointments

Some budgerigars will destroy their eggs as they are laid, and apart from possibly fostering them to another pair, the only possible means of overcoming the problem is to supply an unbreakable dummy canary egg. The mottled appearance of this, contrasting with the budgerigar's white egg, does not cause any problem. Having realized that this egg cannot be destroyed, many hens will then settle down and incubate their other eggs in earnest. Accidental damage to eggs, such as small cracks in the shell can sometimes be successfully repaired with a coat of clear nail varnish. It is a good idea to tap on the nest-box just prior to opening the inspection hatch. This gives the hen time to leave the nest, rather than scampering out madly, scattering eggs out of the concave.

A proportion of eggs will always fail to hatch, and some will not have been fertilized. It is possible to check this by holding them up to a bright light to see if they appear clear, in which case they are infertile. Conversely, when the egg is opaque, it indicates that a chick was formed, but died within the shell. There are various possible reasons for such losses, and if the eggs are soiled, bacteria entering via the shell may have been responsible for the chick's death. In the domestic environment, the level of humidity is often too low during the latter part of incubation, so the chick cannot break out of its membranes successfully. Spraying the outside of the nestbox daily, or giving the hen an opportunity to bathe or roll around on damp greenfood, are sensible precautions against losing chicks in this way.

Having hatched, the small, blind and virtually naked chicks are completely helpless, and yet in the space of only three weeks in some cases, they emerge as immature versions of their parents, fully able to fly. Given the fantastic growth rate over this period necessary to ensure such development, it is not surprising that losses often result from giving the parents an inadequate diet. Protein assumes great importance at this time, and extra sources of protein have been mentioned elsewhere. Failure to supply sufficient live food is a common reason for disappointment when breeding waxbills, which become highly insectivorous at this time. It is no coincidence that species that can rear chicks on a very restricted diet, such as the budgerigar, are most commonly bred throughout the world.

Canaries may vary markedly in their abilities to rear chicks, with some hens being dubbed 'poor feeders', which, as the description suggests, is reflected in the low number of offspring reared. Some breeds are better than others in this respect, and for the novice, success will be more likely with Glosters or Borders rather than Norwich Fancy birds, which have a poor reputation in this respect. Cock canaries are often removed to separate quarters prior to the hatching of chicks, because they can interfere, chasing the hen who is not then able to rear the chicks. A double breeding cage with a removable centre partition is therefore useful if the birds have to be separated. It is also possible to run a cock with two hens successfully, but cocks should not be housed together in the presence of hens as they are very likely to persecute each other.

As the chicks grow older, the problem of feather-plucking may become apparent. Budgerigars, lovebirds and lutino cockatiels are most prone to showing this vice, removing the feathers of their chicks from the base of the neck in the first instance. It can become quite severe, with blood scattered around the nestbox along with the emerging feathers. The cause is not clear, but it does appear to be inherited in some cases. It may simply reflect a desire on the part of the hen to nest again, and she attempts to drive the youngsters away, although cocks can also show such behaviour. Sprinkling bitter aloes around the affected areas of the chicks, avoiding the head, will act as a deterrent in some cases, presumably because of the bitter taste, although birds have relatively few taste buds compared to mammals. The chicks are usually reared without difficulty, and the feathers soon regrow once they are away from their parents.

When the chicks are seen to be feeding themselves, it is useful to transfer them to separate accommodation, so they do not hamper the adults' attempts to nest again. Most of the free-breeding species will have two rounds of chicks in a season, given the opportunity, after which nesting facilities should be withdrawn, so they are allowed to recover from the strain of producing a family. There is a risk with some species that earlier youngsters will be attacked by their parents if left with them too long. This applies particularly to the small parrotlets, as well as lovebirds, whereas it is generally safe in the case of finches and canaries.

The youngsters should be offered the same foods which they were consuming alongside their parents, and should not be expected to transfer suddenly to a diet of seed alone. They must be watched closely to ensure there are no difficulties arising from their move, and for young canaries especially, supple branches, never dowelling, should be supplied as perching.

They appear susceptible to a condition known as 'slipped claw' at this time, which arises when the hind claw loses its function and slides forward over the top of the perch, thus crippling the bird. In common with finches, canaries perch with three claws forward, and one gripping the back of the perch, whereas all parrots, as well as toucans, have two toes either side of their perch.

Failure to breed

There are two main reasons for the failure of a known pair of birds to show signs of nesting activities. They may not be in suitable condition, and lack adequate privacy. Even when kept indoors, most birds are more likely to breed during the spring rather than the winter months, and will be conditioned accordingly. Newly-imported individuals are most unlikely to nest until they have moulted out, and are established in their new surroundings.

Lack of breeding stimulus in fit birds is very rarely, if ever, encountered and a close examination of a pair's surroundings may well yield an explanation of their failure to nest. A single pair of budgerigars commonly ignore their nestbox without the stimulus provided by the sound of other individuals in their immediate locality. Many foreign finches will not breed without sufficient privacy, provided by vegetation, so in an open flight equipped with only a nesting site, failures are likely to result.

Colour breeding

In order to produce youngsters of a desired colour, it is necessary to be aware of the genetic factors which will influence the appearance of such mutants. All the characteristics of an individual, including its colour, are determined by genes, located on paired structures known as chromosomes. Each parent effectively contributes one chromosome to each pair, along with its genes, so there are two genes present for each character, and these may differ or correspond, depending on the parents themselves.

In most instances, the native colour, such as Light Green in the case of the budgerigar, is said to be dominant to other colours. This means that when a Light Green is paired to a Sky Blue for example, then all the offspring will be Light Green in appearance. The genetic coding of these youngsters must, however, also contain the colour genes from each parent, so they will possess a Sky Blue as well as a Light Green gene. Such birds cannot be distinguished from a pure Light Green

Pied Zebra Finches. The actual distribution of the pied markings can be very variable.

by sight, in spite of this genetic difference. Only when they themselves are paired with a Sky Blue will the distinction become obvious, as Sky Blue chicks should result in this case.

It is possible to predict the offspring likely to result from a particular pairing by means of the system known as the Punnett Square. This breaks down such genetic characters, arranging them at right angles to each other. It is then a matter of filling in the possible combinations, and interpreting them. Considering the two examples previously mentioned, the genetic make-up of the Light Green is LL, written in large letters because it is dominant, whereas that of the Sky Blue, being recessive, is ll.

Sky Blue

	l	l
L	Ll	Ll
L	Ll	Ll

Light Green

All these chicks are said to be 'split' for Sky Blue, with this distinction being symbolized by an oblique line.

Sky Blue

	l	l
L	Ll	Ll
l	ll	ll

Light Green/Sky Blue

In this case, approximately 50 per cent of the chicks will be Sky Blue, with the remainder again Light Green/Sky Blue. There is no absolute guarantee, however, that the proportions will be as shown, because these do not necessarily hold for an individual pairing. The fusion of sperm and egg occurs randomly.

There are five possible pairings using these characters, with the expected results of a mating between a Recessive Pied Zebra Finch and a Normal form given below:

1 Recessive Pied × Recessive Pied → 100 per cent Recessive Pied.
2 Recessive Pied × Normal → 100 per cent Normal/Recessive Pied.
3 Recessive Pied × Normal/Recessive Pied → 50 per cent Recessive Pied + 50 per cent Normal.
4 Recessive Pied/Normal × Normal → 50 per cent Normal/ Recessive Pied + 50 per cent Normal.
5 Recessive Pied/Normal × Recessive Pied/Normal → 50 per cent Normal/Recessive Pied + 25 per cent Recessive Pied + 25 per cent Normal.

These figures can all be calculated in the same manner as shown above.

There are also colour mutations which occur only on the pair of sex chromosomes responsible primarily for determining the individual's gender. Unlike other pairs, the sex chromosomes are of a differing length in the case of the hen only, referred to as ZY. The Y chromosome is relatively short, and in this case when a colour mutation occurs on the other chromosome, there will be no corresponding gene as the Y portion is not as long. Thus hens cannot be split for a sex-linked trait, and so in this single case, their genetic appearance is bound to correspond to their bodily appearance. Using the Punnett Square system again, the case of a Fawn Zebra Finch hen $(n-)$ paired with a normal cock (NN) is shown with the dash indicating a Y chromosome, and hence a hen bird.

Fawn hen

		n	—
Normal cock	N	Nn	N—
	N	Nn	N—
		cocks	hens

This should produce 50 per cent Normal/Fawn cocks and 50 per cent Normal hens.

The full list of possible pairings is as follows:

1 Fawn cock × Fawn hen → 50 per cent Fawn cocks + 50 per cent Fawn hens.
2 Fawn cock × Normal hen → 50 per cent Fawn hens + 50 per cent Normal/Fawn cocks.

3 Normal cock × Fawn hen → 50 per cent Normal/Fawn cocks + 50 per cent Normal hens.

4 Normal/Fawn cock × Normal hen → 25 per cent Normal cocks + 25 per cent Normal hens + 25 per cent Normal/Fawn cocks + 25 per cent Fawn hens.

5 Normal/Fawn cock × Fawn hen → 25 per cent Normal/Fawn cocks + 25 per cent Normal hens + 25 per cent Fawn cocks + 25 per cent Fawn hens.

There are also some mutations which are themselves dominant to the normal, such as Grey in the case of the budgerigar. The pairings for these birds are given below:

1 Grey (double factor) × Normal → 100 per cent Grey (single factor).

2 Grey (single factor) × Normal → 50 per cent Grey (single factor) + 50 per cent Normal.

3 Grey (single factor) × Grey (double factor) → 50 per cent Grey (single factor) + 50 per cent Grey (double factor).

4 Grey (single factor) × Grey (single factor) → 50 per cent Grey (single factor) + 25 per cent Grey (double factor) + 25 per cent Normal.

5 Grey (double factor) × Grey (double factor) → 100 per cent Grey (double factor).

Once again, single and double factor birds cannot be separated by sight, as they appear identical. Only in the case of incomplete dominance, manifested by the dark factor in the case of the budgerigar, is there a visual distinction between single and double factor birds. Those with a single dark factor are Dark Green or Cobalt, depending on whether the bird is basically green or blue. When two such factors are present, then Olives and Mauves result. The dark factor in itself is not a colour, it merely alters the depth of coloration already existing in the bird.

Crested mutations

Various crested mutations have been established successfully, in species which normally do not possess a crest. They have proved to be dominant, but only single-factor birds are known. This is because there is a lethal factor involved, which renders double-factor individuals non-viable, so they cannot develop successfully. As a result, therefore, crested birds are always paired with normals, and not to each other, which would automatically reduce the number of potential offspring by a quarter. This is the expected percentage of double factor birds from such a pairing.

A basic guide to the mode of inheritance of some of the more readily available mutations:

Mode of Inheritance	Mutation
Autosomal Recessive	White Zebra Finch
	Recessive Silver Zebra Finch
	Recessive Cream Zebra Finch
	Pied Zebra Finch
	Penguin Zebra Finch
	Yellow-beaked Zebra Finch
	Recessive Pied Budgerigar
	Sky Blue Budgerigar
	Yellow Budgerigar
Sex-linked Recessive	Chestnut-flanked White Zebra Finch
	Albino Zebra Finch and Budgerigar
	Dilute Bengalese
	Lutino Budgerigar
	Cinnamon Budgerigar
	Opaline Budgerigar
Dominant	Dominant Silver Zebra Finch
	Dominant Cream Zebra Finch
	Crested (all species)
	Chocolate Bengalese
	Dominant Pied Budgerigar
	Grey Budgerigar

5 Health disorders

The caring owner should not, with a very few exceptions, attempt to treat his sick pet without seeking advice from a veterinary surgeon. Indeed, even if the veterinarian does not possess specialist knowledge in this particular field, most will be able, where considered appropriate, to refer a case to a more experienced colleague. This chapter is not therefore intended to serve as a substitute for veterinary advice. In some countries, such as the UK, the dispensing of antibiotics is restricted to veterinary surgeons, whereas elsewhere, such as in the USA, certain preparations can be purchased in pet stores. However, even if antibiotics are readily available, it still remains important to select the correct treatment for a particular case. Not all antibiotics are effective against all bacteria, and none is currently active in cases of viral infections. Fungal diseases are also very difficult, if not impossible, to cure by means of antibiotic therapy.

Sick birds

A sick bird is relatively easy to recognize, but the symptoms can be similar for a whole host of conditions. A loss of appetite, coupled with depression and inactivity are often the initial signs. There may be other more specific indications. A bird that perches with its beak open, and head raised is likely to be afflicted with a respiratory problem, as is one with soiled or matted feathers around the nostrils. It is useful to make a note of the signs, so that none is overlooked when you consult a vet. Treatment should always be obtained with minimum delay because this can quite often make the difference between a successful recovery, or loss of the patient.

Most pet birds, once established in the home, rarely fall ill, as long as their basic needs are always considered. At the first sign of illness the temperature of their surroundings should be increased, because smaller birds in particular will rapidly lose body heat. They can be transferred in their cage to a position close to a radiator. Even an electric light bulb suspended over them will be helpful. An infra-red heat lamp is best of all. A red bulb will be less disturbing if it has to be left on at night to maintain the temperature.

Modern methods of treatment

Antibiotics used correctly have proved of great help to bird-keepers, but the instructions for dosage must be strictly adhered to because otherwise adverse side-reactions are likely to result. Preparations in the form of powders mixed with drinking water are favoured by many, but there is no guarantee that the bird will drink sufficient of the mixture to have a beneficial effect. Greenfood, and fruit if possible, should be withheld as these both contain a high proportion of water. In severe cases, the drug may need to be administered by injection, or given orally. These latter methods are mainly applicable for the larger species.

Anaesthetics suitable for birds have been produced, and surgery can now be undertaken with a greater degree of safety as a result. X-rays may be used by a veterinarian to confirm a suspected fracture, and fluid replacement therapy is another example of how treatments have progressed.

Beak, claw and cere disorders

Budgerigars are most commonly afflicted with these disorders. Overgrown beaks, when the upper mandible grows right down over the lower, are encountered quite frequently. The cause of the condition is unclear, but it is certainly much rarer in aviary birds, which have more opportunity to gnaw wood. As a precaution, pet budgerigars should have natural branches in their cages.

When the beak becomes distorted, it will need to be cut back, because otherwise the end twists round and prevents the bird from eating successfully. In most cases, repeated clipping proves necessary, about every six to eight weeks, depending on the individual.

An overgrown beak

It is probably preferable to take the bird to a veterinarian, but if it is to be carried out at home, a pair of bone clippers will be required to cut through the tough tissue of the beak. The blood supply, visible as a dark streak running down the centre of the beak must be carefully noted, and then only the tip, where it is no longer visible, should be cut with a clean clip. No bleeding will result, but in some cases, there is haemorrhage into the beak tissue higher up, which shows as a greenish-black patch on the outer surface. There is no means of treatment for this, and it causes the bird no apparent discomfort.

Undershot beaks are seen less often, being simply the reverse of the previous condition, with the lower mandible growing out abnormally. Nest dirt adhering to the soft beak of a young budgerigar may produce this malformation, but in some cases it is an inherited feature. Regular clipping will again be required, for the remainder of the bird's life.

Beak distortions are much less common in other species, but do arise as an adjunct to cockatoo feather disease, which is discussed later. Overgrown claws often occur, especially in pet birds of many species, typically budgerigars, canaries and some finches, such as weavers. The main danger with such claws is that the bird becomes caught up either in its cage or while at liberty in a room, and injures itself further as a result. Claws can be clipped in the same way as beaks, taking care to locate the blood supply. With black claws, this may prove impossible, and so clipping should be carried out very cautiously, to prevent bleeding. Sand tubes resembling the sheets used on the cage floor, fitted round perches may be useful, providing only one is used in a cage, as the hard particles may irritate the feet.

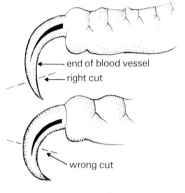

Trimming of overgrown claws must be carried out carefully

Cere changes are again often seen in budgerigars. Hens in fact undergo a normal cycle of colour change, their ceres turning from pale whitish-brown to deep brown in colour as they approach breeding condition. The cere may occasionally become grossly enlarged in some hens and while this is not normally a problem, the bird may have difficulty in breathing if the nostrils become particularly occluded. Enlargement of the nostrils themselves, seen especially in canaries and parrots, is indicative of a chronic sinus disorder, which should receive veterinary attention. Cock budgerigars may, like hens, undergo a change in their cere colour, which becomes brownish, and this is often indicative of a tumour of the reproductive organs, with weight loss also being evident across the breastbone in such cases. If this is the reason, there is not likely to be any possible treatment, and once the bird shows signs of distress, it should be taken to a veterinarian and painlessly euthanased.

There is also a mite, known scientifically as *Cnemidocoptes pilae*, which can infect the beak of budgerigars, spreading to encompass the eyes, and other parts of the body in severe cases. The first signs often resemble a minute snail track, running across the upper beak before large crusty swellings develop. If left untreated, the beak will soon be permanently distorted by the mites, which thankfully can be easily and safely destroyed using a suitable preparation obtainable from pet stores. Liquid treatments, applied to the affected areas with a brush are perhaps most convenient for the purpose. Scaly face may take several years to develop in some cases, with chicks probably being infected in the nest, so it can suddenly appear in a pet

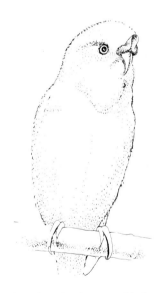

An enlarged or hypertrophied cere

Scaly-face appears around and on the beak itself, but may spread to encompass the eyes if left untreated. It is caused by the mite *Cnemidocoptes*.

Far right Newly-imported lories and lorikeets are prone to *Candida* infections especially if their diet is low in vitamin A. A Mitchell's Lorikeet (*Trichoglossus h. mitchelli*) from the Indonesian islands of Bali and Lombok is shown here.

bird which has no contact with others. A similar mite can affect canaries on their legs, and will respond to the same treatment.

Digestive system disorders

Newly-imported Eclectus parrots, as well as lories and lorikeets, are susceptible to *Candida* infections of the upper part of the digestive tract. This micro-organism, which is related to the yeasts, shows up as whitish colonies in the mouth, and these may extend down the oesophagus into the crop. Treatment is somewhat difficult, but it may respond to specific antibiotic therapy, in conjunction with Vitamin A supplementation.

Crop disorders in budgerigars can be recognized by retching, and a sticky mucoid discharge matting the feathers of the head. It should not be confused with the natural behaviour of cocks, which often attempt to feed mirrors and other toys, and these ought to be removed from the cage for a short period to break their habit.

A bird with crop inflammation often merely dehusks its seed rather than swallowing it, so blackish-brown pieces of canary seed are clearly visible in the food pot. On closer examination, the crop, situated on the left side of the body, just below the neck is often distended with gas. There are various possible causes, and certainly *Candida* appears to be implicated in a number of cases. Recent studies have shown that protozoa can often be found however, and may be the main cause. Treatment is possible, but always be alert since recurrences may occur in some individuals. It is quite often seen in hens that, although in top condition, are not breeding.

Inflammation of the gut, known as enteritis, can affect any species and this may again be caused by a wide range of micro-organisms. Culturing from a fresh faeces sample for the organism concerned is the only positive means of identifying the cause of the problem, and may serve to indicate the most suitable antibiotic. The vent feathering often becomes stained greenish with abnormally coloured and loose faeces, and the bird appears quite ill. Overfeeding with greenfood can produce similar signs but in this case, the bird remains bright. There is little to be gained by attempting treatment with a proprietary remedy, and antibiotic therapy alone is likely to give the best chance of a successful recovery. Enteritis commonly occurs when birds are kept in dirty conditions, or fed seed contaminated by mouse droppings. In severe cases, blood may appear in the faeces, if the protective lining of the gut sloughs off.

Constipation in birds is surprisingly rare, but may follow an attack of enteritis. On average, budgerigars are said to produce

about twenty droppings every day, with the white component equivalent to the urine voided by mammals. The addition of adequate greenfood to the diet of seed-eaters, as well as a supply of adequate grit should eliminate the problem. Where a bird does not pass any droppings for a day, yet appears bright, a capful of olive oil can be mixed in with the seed, in the hope that it will relieve the blockage.

Egg-binding

This complaint is only seen in hens in breeding condition, which are nevertheless unable to expel their eggs. It requires immediate attention. If the bird is placed in a temperature of about 26.5°C (80°F), in a box in an airing cupboard if necessary, the egg may be laid successfully. The problem can often be traced to breeding with young birds too early, and to an inadequate supply of calcium leading to the production of a softshell egg.

Egg-bound hens are often found huddled on the cage floor, and may be paralysed in some cases, although this is usually only transitory. If there is no improvement after a couple of hours in the warm, then the bird must be taken immediately to a veterinarian, who may be able to remove the offending egg by one of several possible means. Birds which recover must not be bred from for at least a year subsequently.

Eye disorders

Eye discharges and swelling may accompany various general illnesses, but if the bird otherwise appears healthy, and particularly when just one eye is affected, it is likely that any infection present is localized, and may have resulted from a slight scratch on the surface of the eye itself. Alternatively, irritants such as a build-up of cigarette smoke in the atmosphere may also lead to eye problems, with the red-eyed varieties of budgerigars being more susceptible than others.

An antibiotic ophthalmic ointment applied three or four times daily will usually clear up an infection rapidly. The eyes are, of course, delicate structures. Only treatments specifically labelled 'ophthalmic' should be used, and no other ointment. In cases of irritation, bathing the eyes with a solution of boracic acid applied on cotton wool can help.

Feather disorders

Parrots kept as pets may well develop the vice of feather-plucking, unless they are receiving adequate attention. Some species are worse in this respect than others, with more intelligent birds such as African Greys most often afflicted. There are various possible causes which may predispose to feather-plucking, but usually there is an associated history of the bird being left alone for long periods, often because it has remained shy, and an inadequate diet comprised just of dry seed.

A rapid alteration to the bird's life-style will be required if this behaviour is not to develop into a habit, with feathers constantly being removed as they grow. Areas of underlying down feathering standing out from normal plumage, typically on the breast, are usually the earliest signs and serve to distinguish this from a normal moult, when there will also be feathers on the cage floor. Some individuals may strip themselves virtually bare over the course of a couple of days, and macaws seem especially bad in this respect.

Aerosol sprays sold to combat feather-plucking rarely help, and should never be viewed as providing a cure, because the initial reason for this behaviour remains untouched. A companion bird of the same species, introduced cautiously, may well solve the problem, and in bad cases, the parrot should also be given access to an outside aviary, providing the weather is favourable. This will often lead to the problem resolving itself, with the bird rarely, if ever, lapsing into its former habit.

Actual feathering abnormalities are also encountered in psittacines more than other species. French Moult, named after the large breeding establishments in France where the complaint was first noted towards the end of the last century, is now a widespread problem, particularly in budgerigars. The symptoms may vary from mild to very severe, in which case all flight and tail feathers fail to develop correctly, and the body plumage remains infantile. The signs in a mild case may hardly be obvious, with perhaps only the loss of a couple of flight feathers, and traces of dark, dried blood visible in the shafts of most of the remainder.

A case of French Moult

With regard to a pet budgerigar, French Moult is probably of little significance, and could even prove an advantage if the bird cannot fly very well, as it will be easier to catch when at liberty. The budgerigar otherwise appears quite normal, and its lifespan seems unaffected. The subsequent loss of developing flight feathers, if this occurs, can sometimes result in haemorrhage.

The disease first appears always in young birds about the time of fledging, and mild cases may later resolve spontaneously. While the disease is still not fully understood, it now appears that it is caused by a virus, although dietary factors may also be involved. No treatment is yet available, but a vaccine may be available in the future.

Back in the 1970s, a feather disease of cockatoos started to be noted. At that stage, it was frequently described as 'Feather Rot'. This is because the feathers typically become brittle, and eventually, the cockatoo is likely to end up quite bald. The beak may soften, and starts to grow abnormally, often splitting.

The cause of this disease has now been identified as a virus and the condition is called Psittacine Beak and Feather Disease (PBFD). This is because it has been identified in over 30 different types of parrot, and not just cockatoos. It can strike at any age.

A vaccine is currently being produced to protect birds against this debilitating and ultimately fatal illness. Once clinical signs develop, there is nothing that can be done in terms of treatment. The bird's condition will continue to deteriorate, to the extent that it may develop other infections, such as candidiasis in its mouth. Great care needs to be taken when cutting the beak, although this is likely to be necessary to allow the bird to continue eating. In the terminal stages, you may need to provide soft food, or dehulled seeds, if the bird is unable to eat properly with its weakened bill.

Great care needs to be taken with a parrot suffering from PBPD, because it can be easily spread. Diagnosis of this illness can be confirmed by a blood test.

Some birds do suffer a continual moult throughout the year when they are housed indoors. The effects of this soft-moulting may well prevent a cock canary, for example, from reaching its full potential as a songster. It is brought on by varying temperatures, or perhaps more often in the home by exposing the bird to artificial light for varying lengths of time over a period. A routine of covering the cage at a specific time is therefore recommended, and certainly after a maximum of about twelve hours total light exposure each day.

Fractures and accidental injuries

Sensible precautions, as outlined previously, should be taken to decrease the risk of such injuries, but on occasions, accidents will occur. A bird suddenly flies out in a room when its cage is being cleaned, and fails to appreciate the presence of a pane of glass, becoming concussed in the process. This problem can also arise if a cage is knocked over with the bird inside.

In such cases, there is really no treatment available, apart from keeping the bird as quiet as possible and with minimal handling, transferring it immediately to a darkened location, such as a box lined with paper tissues, for an hour or so until

Far left Lesser Sulphur-crested Cockatoos (*Cacatua sulphurea*) are prone to a feather complaint for which there is no cure at present. Young birds are typically affected; this is a hen bird as can be ascertained from the reddish-brown eye.

hopefully it has recovered. If the injury is to prove fatal, death usually follows within minutes. However, on occasions, although the bird lives, it suffers convulsions and is incoordinated, which, following an accident, are indicative of brain damage. At this stage, veterinary advice should be sought immediately.

Fractures also require professional attention, and must always be suspected if the bird refuses to use one or more of its limbs, especially when there is a palpable degree of swelling as well. Splints are most conveniently used to immobilize fractures, but, where circumstances dictate in larger birds, it may even be possible to repair a bad break under anaesthesia. Surgical pins can then be inserted to hold the shattered ends of the bone together, hopefully ensuring successful healing. Fractures can occur if the bird becomes caught up by its claws and struggles to free itself, or if it is accidentally trapped by a door.

Bleeding may require immediate action on the part of the owner, and for this reason, a styptic pencil as sold for shaving cuts, or alum powder are useful to have in the home. A solution comprised of one teaspoonful of alum, mixed thoroughly in 0.5 litre (1 pint) of cold water applied either directly or on a piece of cotton wool to the wound will stop most minor bleeding, from beaks or claws as well as feathers, which are the most usual sites. Digital pressure is also a useful adjunct to such coagulants and bleeding should stop within a few minutes following the start of treatment. It is most unlikely to cease instantaneously, unless the injury is very minor, and often blood loss appears worse than is actually the case, so the person treating the bird should try to remain calm. There is no truth in the widely-held belief that a bird will die if it loses several drops of blood. Otherwise healthy pigeons, for example, can survive losing 8 per cent of their total bodyweight in the form of blood, and will usually recover following a haemorrhage which reduces their total blood volume to only 30 per cent of the normal level.

Respiratory system disorders

The respiratory system of birds differs from that of a mammal, because in addition to possessing lungs they also have a series of air-sacs which act to assist in the exchange of gases. While pneumonia is rarely seen in birds, inflammation of these air-sacs, referred to as air-sacculitis, appears more commonly. As with digestive tract infections, there are various possible micro-organisms which may be involved, and these where appropriate will respond to antibiotics.

Breathing difficulties may also result from structures pressing on any part of the respiratory system, such as an enlarged thyroid gland which is often seen in the case of budgerigars. Mites too can live within the air-sacs, giving rise to breathing difficulties, and distinguishing between these different causes requires veterinary advice.

Tumours

Budgerigars have an abnormally high incidence of tumours, which, according to various surveys, will afflict at least three out of every ten individuals. These may be benign or malignant, with the reproductive organs and kidneys being commonly diseased organs. Fatty tissue gives rise to lipomas, which, although benign, handicap the bird, often preventing it from flying effectively. Surgical removal of such lumps can be practical, depending on the tumour and its site, so a vet should be consulted without delay, because if left too long, it may then be impossible to operate successfully.

Lumps encountered in Norwich Fancy Canaries often prove to be feather-cysts rather than actual tumours. These occur typically on the wings, and arise from the failure of the feather to break out through the skin, so it becomes trapped and turns in on itself, with internal secretions around it giving rise to a distinct swelling. These eventually rupture, but this is an inherited developmental abnormality, and cannot be cured satisfactorily.

Zoonoses

Zoonoses are diseases which are transmissable from animals to man, and a variety of such diseases have been reported, of which psittacosis or 'parrot fever' is most notorious. This disease can affect any bird, and so now is often referred to as chlamydiosis, being caused by the micro-organism *Chlamydia*. Indeed, very severe outbreaks have occurred during recent years in Eastern Europe in workers connected with the duck industry, while turkeys caused a major outbreak in America.

Chlamydiosis is difficult to diagnose reliably in birds as there are no clear-cut symptoms but it can be confirmed at a post-mortem examination. The average figures over a ten-year period for notified cases in America suggest about forty-six people each year become ill with chlamydiosis, out of which a significant proportion have had no contact with birds whatsoever, while for the whole of Australia there are less than five cases per year. The risk is not therefore as great as some would suggest.

Chlamydiosis produces an illness resembling influenza in its initial stages, which can be fatal especially in older people, but should respond well to tetracyclines if these are given early in the course of the infection. Recently-imported parrots are likely to pose the greatest threat of introducing chlamydiosis into a home and if the bird appears at all ill, then a veterinarian must be contacted at once, because of the possible hazards to human health. He will advise accordingly, and will be able to arrange for tests to be carried out, to discover if the bird is actually suffering from chlamydiosis.

Spread of this disease to humans is usually by inhalation of particles from the droppings. Allergies may also develop following repeated exposure to dried bird excrement and feather dust, which is associated particularly with cockatoos. Daily spraying will help to damp down this dust, so there is less atmospheric contamination, which is the major precipitating factor in such allergies. Skin tests can be used to confirm this problem, and if in doubt, medical advice should be sought, as for chlamydiosis.

6 Birds kept for their song and colour

Canaries are regarded as the best songsters, compared to other seed-eaters, with some breeds having been bred especially for their singing ability. Others have been produced to conform to prescribed exhibition standards, while a third group are comprised of birds bred primarily for their coloration. All the various breeds of canary are thought to have descended from finches occurring on islands located off the north-western coast of Africa. These wild canaries are basically green, and quite small, being approximately 11 cm (4½ in) long, compared to today's breeds.

The Portuguese are credited with introducing canaries to Europe, during the fifteenth century. The origin of yellow canaries is said to have resulted following a storm at sea, which forced the crew to liberate their birds. These then hybridized with the finches occurring on the nearest island. Several centuries later, the introduction of another finch, the Black-hooded Red Siskin (*Carduelis cucullatus*), to canary bloodlines was to give rise to Red Factor birds.

While pet canaries are kept especially for their singing ability, a few individuals have learnt to talk successfully. A hand-reared youngster bred by Mrs Steer in North Devon, England during 1980 was housed in a separate cage adjoining her pet budgerigar 'Joey'. By the age of three months this canary could repeat the bird's name, as well as referring to it as cheeky!

In Germany, the development of the canary's song began in earnest, especially around the district of the Hartz Mountains. By the seventeenth century, the birds were widely recognized as being superior songsters to wild canaries. They were frequently trained to develop a song pattern resembling the bubbling noise of the streams running down the mountainsides of the region. This initial training has been perpetuated right down to the present day, with a 'Deep Bubbling Water Tour' still included as part of their song schedule at exhibitions.

Rollers do in fact require training to develop into disciplined songsters, able to meet the demands of a singing contest where various recognized 'tours' and 'rolls' must be performed, and

Above Wild serins were the main ancestors of all today's canary breeds.

Above right Uncrested and crested Glosters – known as Consorts and Coronas respectively.

Right Frilled Canaries.

Below Hybrid of Canary × Goldfinch. These birds, called mules, make good songsters.

A white canary.

are marked accordingly. Kept as pets, however, they will still prove to be free singers, and breed quite easily.

In the USA during recent years, a separate breed has been created primarily for its song, being known as the American Singer. Roller blood has contributed over two-thirds of its pedigree, while the Border Fancy has also been used to develop the bloodline. The origins of the American Singer can be traced back to 1934, and subsequently it has become a popular house pet, as well as an exhibition bird. These canaries are not currently being bred in Europe at present, where the Roller still reigns supreme as a songster.

Two of the most popular exhibition breeds today are the Border Fancy and the Gloster Fancy. Cock birds will sing, but do not rival the previous varieties in this respect. Border Canaries originated in Scotland, and then became known as Cumberland Canaries around the Lake District of England. Having been known in Scotland as Common Canaries, the breeders decided on the compromise name of Border Fancy during 1890, seventy years after the breed first appeared. They are now available in a wide range of colours, ranging from white and yellow to green and cinnamon.

Although initially known as the 'Wee Gem' because of its small size, Borders have become bigger in recent years. As a result, some breeders then aimed to produce birds which were more faithful replicas of the original Border. This quest began in 1957, and now the Fife Fancy is firmly established, being widely-kept in many countries. These birds are miniature Borders, being approximately 11.25 cm (4¼in) in length, which is about 2.5 cm (1 in) shorter than their average fore-runner.

The Gloster Fancy Canary, as with some other breeds, is named after the English county where it originated, during the 1920s. The crest of Coronas was achieved by using Crested Rollers, and breeding these with Border Canaries. The non-crested or plainhead variety is known as the Consort. Pairs should, as with other crested birds, be comprised of one bird of each type, to breed the maximum number of crested off-spring.

Breeding canaries

Either Borders or Glosters, apart from Fife Fancies provide a very suitable introduction to breeding canaries. They make quite reliable parents as a general rule, and are even used for fostering purposes by breeders of some other varieties which are less satisfactory in this respect. There is no obvious difference between the sexes, apart from the cock's song, until the birds come into breeding condition. Then if the vent region is examined by blowing the feathers aside, this area is seen to be slightly enlarged in the case of the cock, but relatively flat in hens. The incubation period for canaries is thirteen days, and the youngsters fledge when about three weeks old.

Other type breeds

The Lizard is probably the oldest known breed now in existence, being recognized as early as 1709, when the first list of varieties was produced, and it has changed little down the intervening centuries. Lizards, with their regular speckled plumage supposedly resembling the scaling seen in such reptiles, have a prominent 'cap' in many cases. This is the clear unmarked area on the top of the head, which may be broken into two parts, and then the bird is spoken of as being 'Broken-capped'. Those without caps are referred to as 'Non-caps'.

Lizard Canaries are divided into gold and silver, which is suggestive of colour, but in fact refers primarily to their feather structure. In all breeds, two distinctive types of feathering are recognized, being known as buff and yellow, which correspond to silver and gold respectively in the case of the Lizard. Buff-feathered birds are paler than their yellow counterparts, because the pigment responsible for such coloration is not found at the tips of the individual feathers, which are thus white. This gives the canary a frosted or silver appearance overall, seen most obviously around the head region. The feather structure is somewhat different, being softer in the case of a Buff, so that these birds may appear slightly bigger than yellows.

When breeding canaries, it is usual to pair a buff with a yellow, to prevent any deterioration in the quality of the youngsters' plumage over subsequent generations. The effects of constantly pairing yellows together can be seen in the case of the *Gibber Italicus*, which is of Italian origin. There is no buff form, and so these birds now have rather thin plumage, with no feathering at all on their thighs or breastbone, as yellows have been paired constantly together.

The reverse effect is seen in Norwich Canaries, known affectionately as the 'John Bull' variety, after the stocky character of English folklore. These birds are still especially popular in the East Anglian region, where their ancestors were introduced by Flemish weavers, escaping from the continent in the face of religious persecution several centuries ago.

About 1881, Norwich Canaries, which were much bigger than any previously seen in their home region, appeared from northern England. These resulted from pairing buff to buff

Above right New Colour Canaries are available in a whole range of shades and colours.

Zebra Finches (*Taeniopygia guttata*) are named after the characteristic barring seen on the chests of cock birds.

Above left Mannikins or nuns are the ancestors of the Bengalese Finch, as well as being popular in their own right.

The Sharp-tailed Munia (*Lonchura striata acuticauda*) is thought to have contributed to the ancestry of the Bengalese Finch.

(known in the Fancy as 'double buffing') over numerous generations, and suffered in many cases not only from coarse feathering but were also afflicted with feather 'lumps' or cysts. This fault remains with the breed right down to the present day, and cannot be cured, because it is a defect which affects the structure of the plumage itself.

Other breeds have also changed dramatically in their shape down the centuries. Early Yorkshire Canaries being very slim, were popularly regarded as being able to slide through a wedding ring. This feature is now much less pronounced, although these canaries are still amongst the longest, reaching 17.5 cm (7 in) in some cases.

While some of the older varieties, such as the London Fancy, have been lost, much interest has been rekindled in such breeds during recent years, and so greater numbers are now seen at the larger shows. Scotch Fancy Canaries for example, which contributed to the parentage of the Yorkshire, have undergone a welcome revival. There are also other breeds, seen more commonly in Europe, including the various Frilled Canaries, such as the *Gibber Italicus* previously mentioned. Their frilled plumage is divided into three basic arrangements, with individual variations depending on the type concerned.

The most significant development in canaries during the present century also had its origins in Europe, where the first New Colour birds were produced. There remains a difference in the nomenclature for these birds, however, depending on the country concerned. Over fifty different colour types are now known, of which the Red Factor birds have proved most popular. These arose from crossings with the Hooded Siskin, following the suggestion of the geneticist Dr Duncker that such pairings should lead to the production of red canaries. Unfortunately, his theory did not prove completely accurate, but deep orange-red birds have eventually resulted from such pairings.

The first generation offspring were copper in colour, and all hens produced were infertile. It took three generations, mating these hybrids back to canaries, in order to overcome the problem of infertility in the hybrid hens. Unlike most other breeds of canary, Red Factors are generally clear birds rather than variegated, which show patches of darker markings. They are without doubt the most colourful canaries, but do require colour feeding to maximize the depth of coloration in their plumage.

Canaries will also hybridize with other finches, and the resulting offspring are known as mules. It is usually necessary to cross a cock finch, such as a Goldfinch (*Carduelis carduelis*) with a hen canary to achieve fertile eggs, but a noted exception is the Bullfinch, where a male canary is required. Such mules, although infertile, do generally prove to be good songsters.

Zebra Finches (*Taeniopygia guttata castanotis*)

These little Australian finches, about 11 cm (4½ in) in length, were known in Europe by 1805, and reproducing freely in aviaries by 1872. Their popularity has not waned subsequently, and today they are the most widely-kept small seedeaters worldwide. Zebra Finches take their name from the characteristic black and white barring seen in the case of normal cocks. This variety, also referred to as the Grey because of its head coloration, can be sexed without difficulty. Cocks have circular patches of orange feathering extending downwards from below the eyes, and chestnut flanks which are spotted white. These characteristics are not seen in Grey hens, which also have paler red beaks.

It is not, however, possible to sex all the resulting mutations so easily. In the case of the White, bred initially in Sydney, Australia, during 1921, both sexes are pure white, with only the difference in beak coloration to separate them visually. The same distinction between the sexes is also seen in Albino Zebra Finches, which although pure white, have red eyes.

While the early Whites often had some dark feathers, a separate distinct Pied mutation occurred in Denmark about 1936. In the case of the Grey Pied, birds with variable areas of white, replacing the usual markings are seen, but the pied factor can also be combined with other colours, such as Fawn. The Fawn or Cinnamon mutation itself originated in Australia about 1927, and causes the plumage to be light brown, instead of grey.

Some of these mutants do occur in the wild, and the Chestnut-flanked White was established from some wild-caught individuals. As their name suggests, these birds retain their flank markings in the case of the cock, while being predominantly white. Hens can be distinguished from White females because they retain the dark line running down from the eyes, and tail barring, which is never present in the case of the latter variety.

Penguin Zebra Finches have lost the characteristic zebra marking seen in cocks of other varieties, and so their underparts right from the lower beak are white. The effect can be combined with all colours, but is most striking in Grey and Fawn birds. Another mutation which can be superimposed on these two colours is a diluting character, which leads to the production of Silvers and Creams respectively. There are both recessive and dominant forms, which have occurred separately.

Above Fawn and White Bengalese (*Lonchura domestica*).

The Spice Bird or Nutmeg Finch (*Lonchura punctulata*) is a native of South-east Asia.

Amongst the other rarer mutations, Crested Zebra Finches were first identified in Spain during the late 1960s. As in other species, this can be added to any chosen colour form. The Yellow-beaked variety is also increasing in numbers, while Black-breasted Zebras are currently becoming more widespread as well. In time, other new mutations can be expected to occur with pure Black Zebra Finches already recorded.

Above An African Silverbill (*Euodice malabarica cantans*). An Indian form is also recognized.

Left St Helena Waxbill (*Estrilda astrild*).

Below left A pair of Gold-breasted Waxbills (*Amandava subflava*). The hen is seen on the left.

Breeding notes These finches generally prove quite free-breeding in the home, although their persistent cheeping call can become monotonous when heard at close quarters. The incubation period is approximately twelve days and the youngsters fledge at the age of about two and a half weeks, being independent within another ten days. They should then be separated, as the adults will probably want to breed again, and may turn on their early offspring, especially in the confines of a cage.

Bengalese Finches (*Lonchura domestica*)

These finches are somewhat of an oddity because they form a hybrid race, and thus are not found in a wild state. Various suggestions have been made about their ancestry, and it seems most likely that they originated from crossings using the Sharp-tailed or White-rumped Mannikin (*Lonchura striata acuticauda*) or perhaps a related subspecies, the Striated Mannikin. The noted zoologist, Dr Desmond Morris, could find no evidence of behavioural similarities between Bengalese and Silverbills (*Euodice* species), another possible ancestor, which tends to suggest that these finches were not involved to any great extent in the breed's origins. Bengalese were first produced in the Orient, over two centuries ago, either in Japan or China, and are now available in a variety of colour forms.

The Chocolate variety is dark brown, whereas the Fawn is a lighter brown. Pied forms of both these colours are also bred, and such birds are often described as variegated, in contrast to the self, which is the pure colour. A dilute form of the chocolate is sometimes seen, and may initially resemble a Fawn, although it lacks the red eyes associated with the latter variety. A white mutation has also been bred, and such birds were the first Bengalese to be seen in Europe, when a pair arrived at London Zoo during 1860. They have, however, remained rather scarce, and are generally smaller than other colours.

Bengalese are still very popular in the Far East, and a crested strain was evolved in Japan, having a full circular crest. Frilled varieties, however, are still rare outside Japan, but can be seen occasionally as can Tri-coloured individuals. Birds of this latter type have regions of chocolate, white and fawn feathering on their bodies, but it does not seem possible to transmit this characteristic to the next generation.

Breeding notes Bengalese can only be sexed when in breeding condition, and like the Zebra Finch, they have an incubation period of twelve days. The chicks fledge when approximately three weeks old. Perhaps because of their role of acting foster parents for other species, Bengalese are also referred to as Society Finches, particularly in the USA.

Foreign Mannikins

These birds lack the bright coloration associated with some foreign finches such as waxbills, and are quite stocky in appearance. The White-headed Nun (*Lonchura maja*) from Malaysia is often available, as is the related Black-headed form (*L. atricapilla*). Apart from being referred to as Nuns, these Mannikins are also sometimes advertised using their old generic name, Munia. The Spice Bird, (*L. punctulata*) occurring in India, is another member of this group. Other Mannikins, such as the Magpie Mannikin (*Spermestes fringilloides*), are found in parts of Africa.

Breeding notes Like the Bengalese, these finches cannot be sexed easily, and in addition do not prove very prolific breeders. The incubation period is about thirteen days, with the young leaving the nest at three and a half weeks of age. They only acquire adult plumage when four months old, and prior to this, are generally duller than their parents.

Although they are usually immaculate, particularly when given an opportunity to bathe, these finches often suffer from overgrown claws, which must be cut back regularly. They would appear to have a long lifespan, with some individuals living to fifteen years of age. Nuns will live alongside other finches in harmony, especially Java Sparrows and birds of a similar size.

Silverbills

There are both Indian and African races of these predominantly brown finches. They can be distinguished because the Indian Silverbill (*Euodice m. malabarica*) has a white rather than brown rump. Although sexes appear similar, cocks will sing when in breeding condition as in the case of Mannikins. A group will live together quite satisfactorily, and pairs will nest quite often, laying up to ten eggs at a time. As with imported birds of all species, however, a pair may not start breeding for some months at first. But once they have settled in prove prolific.

Their incubation period is eleven days, with the chicks being black when they hatch. After nearly three weeks, young Silverbills leave the nest and are independent within a further fortnight. Although it is possible to hybridize the two races, this should be avoided whenever possible.

Cordon Bleus (*Uraeginthus bengalus*) can live for fifteen years or more.

The Lavender Finch (*Estrilda caerulescens*) is in fact a Waxbill, belonging to the genus *Estrilda*.

Far right Green Singing Finches (*Serinus mozambicus*) are quite talented songsters, and may breed in the home.

Waxbills

The waxbills are confined largely to Africa and some off-shore islands. Some species, such as the Violet-eared (*Uraeginthus granatina*) are highly prized, but cannot be kept successfully without an adequate supply of livefood. A wide number of species may be seen, and these are generally similar in their habits and requirements, being about 10 cm (4 in) in length.

The most commonly available waxbill is probably the Red-eared (*Estrilda troglodytes*), found over north-east and western Africa. There are, however, other species which have similar red markings extending in a band from the beak to include the eyes, back to the sides of the neck. Sundervall's Waxbill (*E. rhodopyga*) also has a red rump, and the St Helena Waxbill (*E. astrild*) possesses a whitish throat. The rest of their plumage is brownish. Red-eared Waxbills cannot be sexed easily, although at breeding time the cocks develop more pinkish abdomens than hens. They display by holding lengths of grass in their beaks, and require secluded quarters if breeding is to be successful. A similar distinction can be seen in the case of the cock St Helena Waxbills, whereas male Sundevall's Waxbills have darker feathers on the underside of the tail.

The Gold-breasted Waxbill (*Amandava subflava*) is an attractive species, which can be sexed on sight. Hens are duller than cocks, which have orangish underparts, and lack the red stripes above the eyes. Orange-cheeked Waxbills (*E. melpoda*), with their prominent orange markings on the sides of their faces are relatively common, with hens having paler patches. Lavender Finches (*E. caerulescens*) are not called waxbills, because their beaks are black rather than reddish, but prove similar in their habits. Cocks in this case can be recognized by their song, as well as their darker coloration. They do tend to fight amongst themselves, and so each pair should be given separate accommodation, although they can be kept safely alongside related species.

The Cordon Bleu (*Uraeginthus bengalus*) is an attractive waxbill with its sky blue cheeks, chest and tail. The remainder of the plumage is predominantly fawn brown, apart from its crimson ear coverts, which are absent in hen birds. Other species which are similar in appearance include the Blue-headed Waxbill (*U. cyanocephalus*), and the Blue-breasted Waxbill (*U. angolensis*). These are often difficult birds to establish successfully, but once this stage is passed, they may reach an age of fifteen years or more.

Breeding notes Waxbills will not often breed successfully in the home, unless kept in a planted flight, because they need adequate privacy at this time. The incubation period is about twelve days with the youngsters flying for the first time when just under three weeks old. Without a constant supply of suitable insects, chicks will not be reared to maturity.

Finches which sing well

The two species of Singing Finch are, as their name suggests, quite talented songsters, although not really comparable in this respect with the canary itself. The Green species (*Serinus mozambicus*) is most attractive, with yellow plumage on the head and breast, and a darker green back. Hens are generally paler than cocks, which make the best songsters. They have also proved quite prolific breeders, with similar requirements to waxbills. Singing Finches may even breed using canary nest pans. The Grey Singing Finch (*S. leucopygius*) is also available on occasions, and although less colourful than the previous race, can also sing well, and individuals may live for more than two decades.

Various Serins are also occasionally encountered, and these birds will make good songsters. They may sometimes be advertised under the description of canary, to emphasize this feature. The Grey-necked Serin (*Serinus canicollis*), for example, may be referred to as the Cape Canary, which is a native of South Africa. The Golden Song Sparrow (*Passer luteus*) does not have a very impressive voice, however, in spite of its name. These birds are generally wild, and should only be kept in a flight, rather than a cage. The cock is most attractive, with chestnut-brown wings and golden-yellow lower parts, while his mate is dull brown. Breeding results are unlikely unless a colony of these birds are kept. It is interesting that the beak colour of the cock changes to black from brownish when he comes into breeding condition.

Some miscellaneous species

It is impossible to cover the vast number of potential species that may be encountered by the prospective bird-owner. Apart from the more common groups mentioned previously, there are some individual species which are seen on occasions. The Cut-throat (*Amadina fasciata*), so-called because of the red band across its throat, has been bred in captivity repeatedly from 1770 onwards. Hens lack this red marking, apart from being slightly paler overall. The distinction between the sexes can be made while the chicks are still in the nest. Unfortunately, Cut-throats do prove aggressive when breeding, and should never be kept alongside smaller birds such as waxbills.

The Cape Canary (*Serinus canicollis*), also known as the Grey-necked Serin.

Far right Zosterops or White-eye (*Zosterops palpebrosa*). These attractive birds do best in a planted flight.

Java Sparrows (*Padda oryzivora*), also known as Rice Birds, cannot be sexed on sight.

Java Sparrows (*Padda oryzivora*) may not be very colourful, but always look immaculate and will live alongside Cut-throats. The normal variety is grey, with a black cap on the head, and white patches below the eye. Pairs appear identical, although cocks will sing occasionally, unlike hens. While this grey form has not proved very prolific, the mutations seem to breed more easily, with Whites being firmly established. A most attractive Fawn variety is widely kept in Australia, and a few examples are now being bred in Europe. These birds are also known as Rice Birds, particularly in America, because they appreciate Paddy Rice as part of their seed mixture.

Out of the smaller nectivores which are usually available, the Indian White-eye or *Zosterops* proves an ideal introduction to this interesting group of birds. Their name originates from the prominent circular areas of white skin around their eyes. They are a very widespread group of birds, with forms ranging throughout Australasia into Africa and even on to the Pacific Islands, including Hawaii. *Zosterops* can be mixed safely with non-aggressive seed eaters, and prove both intelligent and lively. Males also have quite an attractive song. As with all nectivores, they must be given adequate bathing facilities. If a pair go to nest in a planted flight, the chicks should hatch after twelve days' incubation, and may fledge when less than two weeks old, providing the adults receive a constant supply of livefood.

7 Talking birds

For many people seeking a suitable bird for a pet, the appeal of a talking parrot, coupled with its tameness, is often irresistible. The close rapport that can be achieved between such birds and their owners is well-known. Most larger parrots soon learn to associate with a particular person, while remaining somewhat shy and retiring with others. A few even develop a distinct preference for members of one sex. In view of their longevity, parrots could be considered as potential life-time pets, and while this may appear immediately advantageous, it can have its drawbacks.

The demands of such birds on their owners are in turn correspondingly greater than with other species. They must have regular periods of time devoted to them daily, preferably throughout the day rather than just during the evening. It bears repetition here that bored parrots are likely to become unresponsive and begin feather-plucking. The voices of many larger species are very harsh, especially when heard at close quarters, and may well upset neighbours in the immediate vicinity. Regular periods of screeching are commonplace with some species, particularly Amazon Parrots, and prove hard to overcome, but covering the cage may serve to quieten them occasionally. Although relatively intelligent, such parrots cannot comprehend that they should not make a noise, and so scolding or other means of deterring them will have no effect. In fact, hitting the bird on its beak, or throwing water over it at such times are likely to have a very deleterious effect, because it will lose confidence in its owner. Mistreated parrots appear to have a long memory, and seldom, if ever, recover their trust of people.

For many potential owners, therefore, a budgerigar will make a much more suitable pet. They can become prolific talkers, while their natural voice is quite attractive, and not likely to prove disturbing in a room. They are freely available and much less expensive than related parrots, while being bred in a very large range of colours and types. It is thus much easier to obtain a genuine youngster, which should ensure that the bird develops into a good pet.

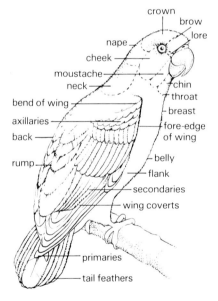

The main points of a bird

A cock Cockatiel (*Nymphicus hollandicus*). Such birds make excellent pets. In Australia, Cockatiels are more commonly known as Quarrions.

Cockatiels have, in recent years, become more appreciated for their qualities as pets, since they have many of the advantages of a cockatoo, which they closely resemble, without its drawbacks in the home. Large numbers are produced annually in aviaries, with colour mutations now also well-established, with the pale yellow Lutino form being most popular.

The only softbill kept for its talking prowess is the Hill Mynah, but its messy habits make it unsuitable for some potential owners. As with similar birds, it is preferable to purchase a young bird, rather than an established talker, which, apart from being more expensive, is also less likely to settle well in new surroundings, and respond to a new owner.

Talking ability in birds

Parrots, although they lack a larynx (responsible for producing the voice in humans) can nevertheless mimic human speech very distinctly. Medical interest in talking birds has grown recently, in the hope that a greater understanding of this ability may help to assist people afflicted with speech disorders, or those who have had their larynx removed.

One of the most interesting recent studies undertaken to investigate whether parrots can actually reason, and thus communicate their thoughts by way of words, was carried out by Irene Pepperberg, a worker in the Department of Biological Sciences at Purdue University, Indiana, USA. She was assisted in this task by Alex, an African Grey obtained in Chicago, who was just over a year old when acquired. With tutoring over the course of the next two years and two months, Alex gained an impressive command of his vocabulary. He learnt three descriptions of colour and was able to refer to shapes by two distinct phrases and mastered nine nouns.

Perhaps most significantly though, Alex was able to use the term 'No' in a meaningful manner, and so could distinguish between over thirty items, which he was also capable of requesting or refusing. Indeed, he would ask for items of his own accord, whether or not they were visible at the time. While such research is still in its infancy, it holds many fascinating possibilities for the future.

Teaching a bird to talk

Teaching a bird to talk successfully requires both time and patience on the part of its owner. In the case of psittacines, the African Grey is considered to make the best pupil, but Amazon Parrots can also prove quite accomplished talkers. Macaws and cockatoos are generally less responsive, but often become equally tame. Lories would also appear to be able to mimic quite successfully, but are rarely kept as pets because of their relatively fluid diet, resulting in their loose droppings.

Young birds of all species, as well as settling in the home quickly, will become better talkers, if given adequate tuition, than older birds. It is not difficult to teach a bird to talk, or even whistle, although some would appear to be more talented in their capabilities than others. Regular repetition of a word or short phrase is required, until the bird mimics this freely of its own accord. By then introducing another suitable word, the bird's vocabulary can be gradually expanded. Providing this is not rushed, the earlier lessons will not be forgotten, especially if they are also repeated at intervals.

Being able to talk can also benefit the bird itself. If an individual can repeat its address, or perhaps a telephone number, it will be much easier for anyone catching the bird, should it ever escape, to contact its owner. This has helped to reunite pets with their mentors on quite a few occasions.

The length of time taken by a bird to start talking will vary, depending on the time spent with it. Aids such as pre-recorded tapes and even records are available in the USA, or can easily be prepared using a cassette tape recorder. These should not be viewed as a means of replacing the human element, which is so vital in teaching the bird to talk, and essential for taming it, with both processes being carried out simultaneously.

In the case of a six week-old budgerigar, it will be quite possible to have the youngster talking by the age of three months old. New phrases can be mastered subsequently, within the space of only a week by some individuals. Their vocabulary should continue growing, with suitable encouragement and even at the age of a year or more, budgerigars can still acquire new phrases if they have been trained effectively straight from the nest. Older birds are most unlikely to start talking, however, and certainly would have a much reduced repertoire.

Finger taming

Taming is again a gradual process, during which time every effort should be made to gain the bird's confidence. It can be fed with pieces of fruit offered by hand at every opportunity, and gradually these will be taken. Parrots like to have the sides and back of their heads tickled, sites which would normally be preened by their mates.

With a new parrot, all such movements should be carried out cautiously, wearing gloves if necessary. It is unlikely that the bird will actually bite if it does not appreciate such advances, being more likely to withdraw to the opposite side of the cage. The trainer will, however, have more confidence using gloves, and sudden disturbing movements close to the bird will be avoided. Once the parrot is perching on the hand, gloves are highly recommended because its claws may well cause inadvertent injury.

When the bird is feeding readily from the hand, with the cage door open, it can then be encouraged to perch on the hand, offering two fingers for large species. Placed parallel to the perch itself, the fingers should be moved slowly and directly over the top of the perch where the bird is sitting. By this means, the parrot should be encouraged to transfer from the perch to the hand, and with constant repetition it will loose all fear of such movement.

The next stage is to persuade the bird to repeat this procedure out of its cage, and hopefully it will remain perching on the hand when it is withdrawn from the cage. Having mastered this step, the parrot can then be allowed to transfer to the shoulder, bearing in mind that even a gentle nip from a macaw is likely to cause severe injury to an ear, for example. At this stage, if not before, the bird should be transferred from its cage to a larger flight unit as recommended previously. Some individuals will even master basic tricks. Parrot Jungle, at Miami, Florida has regular shows featuring performing parrots, which engage in such activities as raising the American flag and answering a telephone. They have also bred in excess of 200 macaws since the park opened in 1936.

The Budgerigar

These parrakeets originate from Australia, and were first seen alive in Britain during 1840, with the pair being brought back by John Gould breeding shortly afterwards, when kept by his brother-in-law, Charles Coxen. They were given the scientific name, *Melopsittacus undulatus*, meaning 'wavy-lined song parrot', reflecting both their bright character and the unique markings on their back and wings. Budgerigars are now the most popular pet birds worldwide, with literally millions being bred annually, both for garden aviaries and exhibition purposes, as well as for pets. Their average lifespan is probably about eight years, but older individuals living into their twenties are not uncommon.

When confronted with a dazzling array of colours, it may be difficult to decide which bird is likely to make the best pet. There is no difference between the varieties with regard to their talking abilities, but Recessive Pieds seem to be slightly less amenable to taming, being more flighty as a general rule. A young bird of about six weeks old, having fledged a week previously and thus being independent of its parents, should already be quite tame, particularly if it was handled in the nest. Most people prefer a cock bird to a hen, thus avoiding possible complications with egg-laying, but either sex can talk, contrary to some opinions. Young cocks are relatively easy to dis-

The wild Budgerigar (*Melopsittacus undulatus*) is light green in colour.

Far left A pair of budgerigars; the hen, with its brown cere, is an opaline, contrasting with the head markings seen in the cock on the right.

tinguish at this age, because they have purplish-pink ceres, which are usually more prominent than those of hens. In the case of hens, their ceres are paler, especially around the nostrils.

A young budgerigar when about six weeks old may still have a dark tip to its beak and completely black or red eyes, depending on the colour concerned. Lutinos and albinos are the most common varieties with red eyes, with lutinos being a deep rich shade of buttercup yellow and thus one of the more popular colours. The markings on the back are not clearly visible in such birds, but in other varieties, the dark lines across the forehead extend additionally right down to the cere itself, giving rise to the alternative name of 'barheads' for baby budgerigars.

When the bird undergoes its first moult, at the age of approximately three months, these markings are partially lost, to be replaced by yellow or white areas of plumage on the forehead, depending on the face colour. Although in most cases the actual body coloration does not change when the bird moults for the first time, the depth of coloration does increase in the case of young Lutinos. The eyes also gain their characteristic irides which are always white and visible round the perimeter of the eye itself. The facial spots, where present, also become larger in most cases.

Apart from Lutinos, Dominant Pied Budgerigars are always popular, with usual shades of blue and white, or green and yellow together. The relative proportions of each colour can vary quite widely between individuals, and on occasions, three

A tufted budgerigar

A half-circular crested budgerigar

A circular-crested budgerigar

Far right The Lutino mutation of the Cockatiel (*Nymphicus hollandicus*) originated in America, and is now widely-kept throughout the world.

colours may be seen on the same bird, with yellow often diluted to pale lemon. Such coloration is perhaps more common in the Recessive Pied, mentioned previously, which originated in Denmark. These pieds are smaller than the Dominant mutation, and never develop irides; their eyes are a very deep plum colour, bordering on black.

Violet budgerigars are an attractive variety, and various shades of blue and green are also seen. The native budgerigar is in fact light green, and this colour is also available, although the export of these parrakeets from Australia has now been prohibited for many years. Other mutations, not actually affecting the body coloration, have also been established, with Opalines being widespread in association with all dark-backed birds. A well-maked Opaline should have a clear V-shaped area on its back, and is inherited as a sex-linked recessive trait. Cinnamons, where these black markings are altered to brown, have also been bred in many colours.

Crested budgerigars have become more widely available during recent years, and three distinct forms are recognized. The Tufted variety has a group of elongated feathers on the head, giving rise to the tuft. The Circular Crested variety resembles Crests seen in Gloster Corona Canaries, being relatively flat and circular, whereas the half-circular form simply has a reduced crest. Crested birds are now being bred in an ever-increasing range of colours, as the crest can be transferred to any desired colour.

Talking prowess Individual birds differ in their abilities. One of the most famous of all talking budgies called 'Sparkie' by his owner, Mrs Williams of Newcastle-upon-Tyne, England, sprang to prominence in a contest organized by the British Broadcasting Corporation during 1958. At the age of four years old, Sparkie Williams beat 2,768 other birds to become a celebrity, appearing on many radio and television programmes of the time. A record of his talking prowess sold no fewer than 20,000 copies worldwide, and he was given virtual immortality by making a disc for the BBC, to be used in cases when a talking budgerigar was called for in a script.

When Sparkie died in 1962, he had mastered no less than 550 individual words, 358 phrases and could even recite eight whole nursery rhymes. Mrs Williams built up his repertoire gradually, by getting him to master two phrases separately and then linking them together. When dealing with nursery rhymes, she encouraged him to repeat the previous verses before continuing with the next so that he never muddled the words. On his death, Sparkie was preserved by a taxidermist, and can be seen at the Hancock Museum, Newcastle.

Breeding details Budgerigars under the age of a year should not be encouraged to breed. They should be fully mature before attempting to raise a family. A clutch may total eight eggs or even more in a few cases, but four is more usual. The hen alone carries out incubation, although the cock may join her in the nest on occasions, and the eggs should hatch eighteen days after being laid. Once the chicks start feathering, a close watch should be kept on their claws and the insides of their beaks, to ensure no nest dirt accumulates here, as it may cause subsequent malformation. The concaves will also need to be changed more frequently as the birds get older.

Keeping a group of budgerigars together will not prevent an individual which talks from using its human vocabulary, but there is an obvious tendency for it to resort to its natural chatter. Teaching a bird which is kept with companions to talk is unlikely to be rewarding.

Sexual problems encountered with single budgerigars
The so-called 'Randy Budgerigar Syndrome' is encountered in cock birds living on their own. They try to mate with mirrors, toys or even an owner's finger. Such behaviour is cyclical, and reflects the frustrated desire of the bird to breed, with some individuals being much worse than others in this respect. The only means of overcoming the problem is to give the bird suitable opportunity to breed, by cautiously introducing a female, together with a breeding cage.

Hen budgerigars kept alone may often produce eggs, which will obviously be infertile. It is inadvisable to remove such eggs immediately, as this may simply stimulate further laying. One hen is recorded as having laid in excess of 200 eggs and such an output obviously causes a drain on the body's resources. If the bird is not to be allowed to breed, she should be left with the eggs and will soon tire of them. Movement to another room may help to prevent the laying of additional eggs.

The Cockatiel (*Nymphicus hollandicus*)

Another native of Australia, the cockatiel is similar in appearance to cockatoos but has a relatively longer tail compared to most species. They are easily sexed because the cock has a yellow head and crest with orange ear patches, while the hen is duller and greyish, although she also possesses the areas of orange on the head. The remainder of the body is largely grey, apart from a prominent area of white on the sides of the wings.

While being popular pets in the USA, cockatiels are only becoming slowly accepted by pet-owners elsewhere, in spite of their many attributes. They are not noisy, cocks having an attractive warbling voice, and they can also learn to talk quite well. As aviary birds, cockatiels have proved relatively prolific, and large numbers of youngsters are available annually at reasonable prices.

It is not possible to sex young cockatiels when they leave the nest, at about five weeks old. The youngsters all resemble adult hens, even possessing the yellow barred undersurfaces to the tail feathers, which is a characteristic of female cockatiels. Immatures can be distinguished, however, by the fact that their tails are relatively short, and their ceres will be pinkish rather than grey. Although cockatiels do not moult until nearly six months old, it is often possible to recognize young cocks from about twelve weeks of age onwards, when they begin to sing.

The ideal time to acquire a young cockatiel is as soon as possible after it is known to be feeding itself. Although more nervous than a budgerigar at this stage, they soon become accustomed to the change in their environment. Given adequate care and training, the young cockatiel should then develop into a delightful pet, with the attributes of a larger parrot, but without the accompanying problems. Most birds will live in excess of two decades, and now with some attractive colour mutations available as well, cockatiels should be given very serious consideration by those seeking a parrot-like bird.

The Lutino mutation, which is also incorrectly referred to on occasions as the Albino or White, originated in the aviaries of Mrs Moon in Florida. Grey coloration is completely lost from birds of this type, while the orange cheek patches are retained. The overall body colour is pale lemon, with some individuals having a darker plumage than others. They can be sexed by the presence or absence of barring on the tail feathers, but need to be examined more closely than normals, because the difference is less obvious.

Pied Cockatiels were the first mutation to be reported, eight years before Lutinos, in 1950, also appearing initially in America, where, like budgerigars, such pied birds are sometimes called Harlequins. They show a similar variation in the degree of piedness, with some individuals being predominantly grey while others are largely whitish.

Amongst the other mutations, the Pearl has become quite widespread, but this scalloped appearance is only temporary in the case of cocks. They produce a greater amount of the pigment melanin, responsible for the coloration of the grey plumage, which thus serves to mask the yellow occurring in the centre of the individual feathers. This change in cocks is seen when they moult out, so they resemble normals, apart from a small area of paler feathering under each wing.

Pages 100–101 Peach-faced Lovebirds (*Agapornis roseicollis*) are popular pets in Australia.

Cinnamons are very attractive, having a pale brownish coffee appearance rather than the grey seen in the case of a normal. Other mutations which are now established include the Dominant Silver, and the White-faced, with birds of this type lacking orange cheek patches, as well as having white rather than yellowish facial feathering. Among the colour combinations being bred is a snow white Albino.

Breeding details Although they are unlikely to breed successfully in the home, a nestbox with dimensions of approximately 20 × 30 cm (8 × 12 in) would be suitable for a pair. The incubation period is approximately nineteen days, with both parents sitting in turn. Unfortunately, not all pairs make satisfactory parents, and may often lose their youngest chicks. They appear to resent their nestbox being examined much more than budgerigars do, and this should be borne in mind if a pair do go to nest.

Lovebirds (*Agapornis* species)

These small short-tailed parrots from Africa have enjoyed a great boom in popularity amongst aviculturists during recent years, and a large number of mutations and colour forms have now been bred. Although not regarded highly as pet birds in Europe or America, they have become popular for this purpose in Australia. With an import ban having been in force here until recently, large foreign parrots became virtually unknown, but Peach-faced Lovebirds thrived in aviaries surroundings, becoming very common here. Young birds can make delightful pets, but they are not talented talkers.

Breeding details Lovebirds construct a nest, which may range from the simple pad used by the Abyssinian (*A. taranta*) to the hooded structure built by White eye-ringed species such as the Masked (*A. personata*). Suitable material in the form of branches with leaves attached must be available to them. The rare Red-faced Lovebird (*A. pullaria*) differs somewhat from other members of the genus, because it breeds in arboreal termite nests.

Pairs should always be given separate accommodation because, as with the majority of psittacines, they are aggressive towards other birds. When provided with a nestbox about 18 cm (7 in) square and 23 cm (9 in) high, lovebirds may nest, but, especially indoors, they produce a relatively high proportion of chicks which fail to hatch successfully after the incubation period of twenty-three days. Spraying the nestbox as suggested previously may help.

Parrotlets (*Forpus* species)

Parrotlets occur naturally in Central and Southern America, and although generally available, they are not suited to being kept in cages. Even pairs will often fight viciously in such surroundings, in spite of their small size, which rarely exceeds 12.5 cm (5 in). A young baby parrotlet straight from the nest may make a good pet, if kept on its own.

Parrakeets

These birds occur on most of the world's major land masses, and are considered here from this viewpoint. A group confined to South America are referred to as conures, simply because of their old generic name, which was '*Conurus*'. The vast majority will only make suitable pets if obtained at a young age. They can be taught to talk successfully, but are not highly gifted in this respect, while many also have harsh voices. Their chief attribute as pets is their tameness, and most are thus kept individually. While some species, such as the Ring-necked Parrakeet, have proved quite free-breeding in collections, extremely few have been reared in a domestic setting indoors.

Australian Parrakeets These birds make ideal aviary occupants, being colourful, hardy and relatively quiet but have very little to offer the prospective pet-seeker. Their active natures ensure that they do not make satisfactory cage-dwellers, and the majority fail to respond to training, remaining shy and retiring, in spite of being bred in captivity outside Australia for many generations.

South American Parrakeets The *Brotogeris* Parrakeets, such as the Canary-winged (*B. versicolorus*) can, by way of contrast, make delightful pets, with newly-imported youngsters often being finger-tame on arrival at their destinations. Adult specimens generally appear to remain shy, however, in spite of all attempts to overcome their fear. The Canary-winged Parrakeet can be distinguished from the White-winged sub-species at a glance because its overall plumage is lighter, being grass-green rather than olive, with patches of yellow on the wings.

The Orange-flanked or Grey-cheeked Parrakeet (*B. pyrrhopterus*) is another member of this genus, and various accounts of these birds as pets have been written over the years. Back in 1919, Dr Lovell Keays had a very tame cock bird, which accompanied him outside but suddenly took fright one day, and flew into an 800 acre forest. Luckily in this case, the parrakeet came back when it was called, which was a great

Right Parrotlets often fight viciously
if kept in cages together. Two
Guiana Parrotlets (*Forpus passerinus*)
are shown here.

Below Sun Conures (*Aratinga
solstitialis*).

Below right A Golden-crowned
Conure (*Aratinga aurea*).

relief to its owner. There is no indication of the age such birds may attain, but fifteen years is not unknown.

Their major drawback as pets is the persistent harsh call which they use when alarmed or jealous, with Canary-wings probably being the worst offenders in this respect. They appreciate the company of another individual, but should be purchased as a pair from the outset, because introducing another of these parrakeets later may result in tantrums from the established pet. Tovi (*B. jugularis*) and Tui (*B. sanctithomae*) Parrakeets are occasionally available and have similar habits.

Conures These fall into two main genera, *Aratinga* and *Pyrrhura*. The *Aratinga* species are more commonly available but tend to be quite raucous. The Golden or Queen of Bavaria's Conure (*A. guarouba*), an endangered species, is to many, the most attractive member of the genus, but proves especially noisy. There are three other predominantly yellow species which would appear desirable, but, like the Golden, are very prone to feather-plucking when kept in cages.

The remainder of the group are largely green, with main variations in colour around the head. Petz's Conure (*A. canicularis*) from Mexico is perhaps not surprisingly most widely known in America, whereas the Golden-crowned or Half-moon Conure (*A. aurea*) is more common in Europe. One

Nanday Conures (*Aratinga nendayus*) are extremely vocal.

of these conures, kept by Mr and Mrs Borge in Honolulu, became so tame that it learnt to jig about to the word 'dance', as well as learning to whistle and mimic laughter. Although these two species resemble each other, both with a band of orange on the forehead, they can be distinguished because the Half-moon Conure has a black beak, whereas that of Petz's Conure is more ivory. In the case of immature Half-moon Conures, there is a band of yellow plumage replacing part of the orange of the adult, and the beak is not completely black.

Apart from these two *Aratinga* species, there are a number which have red plumage on the head, to a variable degree, and perhaps elsewhere on the body such as the edges of the wings. Although very similar in their habits, distinguishing between these species is not easy without reference to a specialized text.

While the Nanday or Black-headed Conure (*Nandayus nenday*) is not included with the *Aratingas* by all taxonomists, it is certainly very closely related, as has been shown by successful hybridization between the two groups. These conures can be very noisy, and destructive, although hand-reared individuals are said to be better in this respect, and settle quite well as pets. It occurs widely over much of central-southern South America, where flocks cause considerable damage to crops of maize and sunflower.

The Quaker or Monk Parrakeet (*Myiopsitta monachus*) is often seen alongside the Nanday Conure, and is likely to prove equally noisy as a pet. These birds have the interesting habit of building large community nests comprised of sticks, rather than adopting tree hollows as nesting sites. During recent years, Quaker Parrakeets have even become established in parts of north-eastern America, although they have been eradicated from New York. Predominantly green, these parrakeets are rather attractive with grey forehead and cheeks, becoming browner on the breast and underparts. They are about the same size as the *Aratinga* conures, being nearly 30 cm (12 in) in length.

The only member of the *Pyrrhura* genus encountered commonly is variously known as the Maroon or Red-bellied Conure (*P. frontalis*). A subspecies, known as Azara's Conure (*P. f. chiripepe*) is also advertised on occasions. These conures do make delightful pets and, even if wild when first obtained, the vast majority, given adequate time, settle and are soon feeding from the hand. Their appearance is also attractive, with deep jungle green wings, brown ear patches and a broad band of deep reddish plumage between the legs.

This whole group of conures is unmistakeable, because of their so-called scaly-breasted appearance, which is yellowish-brown in this particular instance. Like the other South

American species, these conures cannot be sexed by sight, but true pairs prove prolific, rearing as many as six youngsters without difficulty, providing they are given an adequate diet.

Red-bellied Conures may well learn to talk successfully, and their voices are not unpleasant, consisting largely of a 'clacking' sound. Their inquisitive natures, coupled with their friendliness, make them the most desirable of parrakeet species.

The only remaining genus not covered, but examples of which are sometimes seen is *Cyanoliseus*, comprised of *C. patagonus* only. The Patagonian Conure is in fact the largest of the South American conures, and although a very attractive bird, is perhaps even more noisy and destructive than other species. Young birds, recognized by their white beaks, can be kept as pets, and will learn a few words of speech if these faults are considered first. The vast majority are passionately fond of cuttlefish bone, which should always be available.

Asiatic and African parrakeets The genus *Psittacula* has representatives on both continents. The Ring-necked Parrakeet (*P. krameri*), which occurs both in India and Africa is the most-widely kept member of the group. The Indian form (*P. k. manillensis*) can be distinguished from the rarer African race (*P. k. krameri*) because it is larger and has a paler red upper mandible. These birds have an even wider distribution, with colonies established in parts of south-east England, where they are assisted in their hunt for food during the winter by bird-table offerings. It is unlikely, without such help, that they would be able to survive in the UK.

Ring-neck Parrakeets are a beautiful grass green, with a long tapering tail, taking their total length to approximately 40 cm (15 in). Cocks have a colourful nuchal collar, comprised of a band of black edged with pink either side of the neck. They obtain this collar when about two and a half years old, perhaps a year earlier in a few cases, which is a useful means of recognizing an older individual. Unfortunately, these older birds are sometimes offered as youngsters to unsuspecting people, often at a bargain price.

Genuine youngsters, which should make good pets, can be identified by means of their paler bills, and much shorter tails. Various colour mutations have been bred, with Blues and Lutinos most common at present, but these are still rather expensive. It can take a long time to establish such colours though, because these parrakeets may not breed for the first time until their third year.

The similar but larger Alexandrine Parrakeet (*P. eupatria*) can be distinguished by the red patches on its wing, which are never seen in the case of the Ring-neck. Hens in particular have

Above Moustached Parrakeets (*Psittacula alexandri*) are now less common.

Above right A Patagonian Conure (*Cyanoliseus patagonus*). An attractive but noisy species.

Below A cock Alexandrine Parrakeet (*Psittacula eupatria*).

a powerful voice, and can learn to speak a few words. They may make delightful pets, as Edward Boosey, founder of the famous Keston Bird Farm, recollected about a savage individual he was warned not to touch when visiting another pioneering aviculturist Lord Tavistock, later to become the Duke of Bedford.

From this unpromising introduction, the cock Alexandrine took immediately to Boosey, and subsequently he was given the bird. Once home, it lived at liberty, flying into Boosey's bedroom each morning, until it started destroying the wardrobe. The Alexandrine nevertheless remained devoted to Boosey, flying on to his shoulder whenever he ventured out of the house. Boosey was forced to move, however, and rather than cage his pet, he sent the Alexandrine with its mate back to Lord Tavistock. While in these new surroundings, it sadly met an untimely end, being shot while flying free.

Out of the remaining members of the genus, only the Moustached Parrakeet (*P. alexandri*) is really suitable for consideration as a pet, but has become much more rarely available during recent years. These parrakeets often prove difficult to establish, and have loud calls. The related Plum-head Parrakeet generally remains very shy, and even youngsters will not make satisfactory pets.

A Senegal Parrot (*Poicephalus senegalus*). Young birds only should be considered as potential pets.

Poicephalus Parrots

This group of medium-sized short-tailed parrots are quite colourful in the case of the more common species, but unless obtained young, will prove to be very disappointing pets. The Senegal Parrot (*P. senegalus*) is often advertised, and is green on the wings with a greyish-black head and yellowish underparts, which can verge on reddish in the case of one subspecies. These parrots occur in a wide belt of country extending from western to central Africa, through Senegal itself. Young birds have dark greyish-brown irides, with a more brownish head than adults. It is thus easy to distinguish a genuine youngster, because in older individuals, the irides become yellowish.

Meyer's Parrot (*P. meyeri*) has a wider distribution, over the majority of central Africa, extending from Ethiopia down to the Transvaal. The irides again serve to distinguish between immatures and adults, as in the latter case they are orange, rather than dark brown. The calls of these birds consist of a series of whistling noises, which are not disturbing. They are generally fond of peanuts, and these prove useful for taming purposes. Breeding results even in aviaries are not common, and the sexes in these two species cannot be distinguished, so a Danish success achieved in 1956 was probably unique. The pair of Senegals concerned adopted a nestbox fixed outside their cage, which was only 45 cm square and 60 cm high (18 in sq and 24 in high) in size, and the hen laid three eggs. Two chicks emerged after an incubation period of twenty five days and one fledged successfully.

Poicephalus Parrots may not prove easy to tame, but such birds can be delightful pets. Edward Boosey kept a pet Senegal for twenty-one years, which delighted in eating boiled white fish. He described her as 'One of the sweetest and tamest things I have ever possessed'. She learnt to speak a little, and whistled his dogs, pausing to laugh at them when they appeared in the room, searching for their absent master. Another equally tame Senegal Parrot provided great comfort for Maud Knobel, when she was ill, as it lay with her in bed for long periods.

African Grey Parrot (*Psittacus erithacus*)

These parrots occur in central Africa, extending eastwards beyond Lake Victoria, and may even be on the increase in some areas. They are grey apart from the tail, which is bright red. A subspecies known as the Timneh Grey Parrot (*P. e. timneh*), confined to the western part of their range, is darker overall with a maroon tail. This race generally commands a much lower price, and yet is equally satisfactory as a pet. Some dealers advertise 'Silver Greys', which are somewhat paler than usual, and these often originate from Zaire.

Greys have been popular pets for centuries, dating back to the reign of Henry VIII, and a close association between these birds and sailors can be found in writings of previous centuries. An author in 1868 complained that these parrots were deliberately taught unseemly phrases by sailors on the journey back from Africa, and then sold to unsuspecting individuals when the ship reached port. In spite of all subsequent attempts at moral training, these birds relapsed into their former vulgarities at intervals! Indeed, once a parrot has learnt to swear, it is virtually impossible to persuade it to drop the offending words from its vocabulary.

While adult Greys are shy by nature, being known as 'Growlers' because of the noise they emit, usually from the cage floor, when someone is close at hand, young birds can easily be recognized. Once again, the irides reveal the characteristic difference as they are greyish in youngsters and yellow in older birds. Hand-reared chicks are usually available.

American Parrots

The Amazons, sometimes known as 'Green Parrots', are most commonly kept as pets. However, there are smaller and less noisy species which may well prove more suitable. Two members of the genus *Pionus* are often available, and these are the Maximilian's (*P. maximiliani*) and Blue-headed (*P. menstruus*) Parrots. Both species are predominantly dark green in colour, with red feathers on the underside of the tail. The Blue-headed Parrot as its name suggests has a dark blue head, with deep brown ear coverts.

As pets, these parrots are much safer for children to handle than larger species. When hand-reared, they can make superb companions, as shown by Hector, a Blue-headed Parrot bred in Hampshire. On his way to Spain from Britain, Hector accompanied his young owner Pablo around Heathrow Airport perching on his shoulder, and even paused to enjoy a meal of tinned sweetcorn, unperturbed by the surrounding hustle in the departure lounge. Immature Blue-headed Parrots can be recognized because they have a red band across the forehead, and lack the blue markings seen in adults. They occur naturally over much of northern South America, ranging down to Bolivia and Brazil.

Amazon Parrots

There are twenty-four species of Amazon Parrot occurring in Central and South America, as well as on some off-shore islands. These latter populations in particular are causing great concern to conservationists, as their numbers are showing a serious decline in some cases. The species found in Puerto Rico is comprised of about forty individuals in the wild, with a similar number forming part of a captive-breeding project to increase their numbers. Sadly however, it could be too late to save the Puerto Rican Amazon.

Other species, formerly common in parts of their range, are also becoming much scarcer. The Double Yellow-headed Amazon (*A. ochrocephala*), several races of which are recognized, is a member of this group. These parrots are popular pets in America especially, in spite of their loud voice. Two other species of Amazon often available are still quite widespread over much of the northern part of South America. Both the Blue-fronted (*A. aestiva*) and the Orange-winged (*A. amazonica*) appear to have been less affected by deforestation than the previous species. The clearing of large tracts of forest is the major factor leading to the decline in numbers of many birds from this continent.

The Blue-fronted Amazon has a characteristic area of blue directly above the beak, the remainder of the face being yellow. The shoulder edges of the wings are edged with red, while the secondary flight feathers are also red. The Orange-winged species may initially appear similar, but is smaller, rarely exceeding 33cm (13in) in length. It lacks the red at the bend of the wing, and orange replaces red elsewhere. The markings on the head vary quite widely in individuals of both species, and cannot be taken as an indication of the bird's sex.

The small White-fronted Amazon (*A. albifrons*) is in fact a more northerly species, occurring in Mexico southwards to Costa Rica. Hens generally lack the red markings seen on the wings of cocks. Young birds cannot be distinguished by this means, however, as both sexes have green wings. Immatures can also be recognized because they do not possess a complete circle of red plumage around the eyes, while the white band on their heads is reduced and often tinged with yellow. The remainder of the feathering is largely dark green, as in the case of the other Amazons discussed previously. White-fronted Amazons can make most attractive pets.

When choosing an Amazon for a pet, only young birds should be considered. The irides are dark brown at this age, and the birds are generally less colourful overall, compared to adults. They may have a long lifespan, with authenticated reports suggesting that Blue-fronted Amazons may live to nearly a century. A most remarkable breeding with this same species was achieved on the floor of a parrot cage during the early 1940s. A pair kept by G. D. Smith of Aberdeen, Scotland, nested repeatedly, with one youngster being reared by means of partial hand-feeding during 1941, followed by further unaided successes both in 1945 and 1946.

A variety of other species of Amazon are occasionally seen, with Mexican races such as the Green-cheeked (*A. viridingenalis*) and the Lilac-crowned (*A. finschi*) most common in America. The area of red plumage extends back over the eyes in the case of the former species, but is replaced by mauvish feathering in birds of the latter species. These parrots are noisy, like all Amazons, and may also develop unreliable temperaments as they mature, but the large and rather dull Mealy Amazon (*A. farinosa*) has perhaps the most powerful voice of the whole of the genus.

Cockatoos

These birds all possess crests, which are raised when the individual is alarmed or excited and this unique feature makes them instantly recognizable. Like the Amazons, some species are found only on certain islands, in this case confined to those north of Australia, and thus have a very limited distribution. The attractive Citron-crested Cockatoo for example occurs exclusively on the small island of Sumba.

Far right A Blue and Gold Macaw (*Ara ararauna*).

The choice of one of these birds as a pet should therefore be considered very carefully, and the vast majority do not settle as well as the cockatiel in a home. Cockatoos tend to be quite highly-strung, and although they will tame if obtained young, they are not talented talkers compared to other psittacines. Without adequate attention, cockatoos rapidly develop into feather-pluckers and their loud harsh voices are a further drawback when they are kept indoors.

With the export of Australian species banned, the Lesser Sulphur-crested Cockatoo (*Cacatua sulphurea*) is the most frequently seen. It is basically white, with a lemon-coloured crest and ear coverts. Adults can be sexed easily by the difference in their eye colours, with hens being brownish-red, while the eyes of cock birds are jet black. This also applies in the case of other members of the group. Young birds are susceptible to 'Feather Rot', and should be examined closely (see page 65).

The Great Sulphur-crested Cockatoo (*C. galerita*) is about 17.5cm (7in) bigger than the Lesser variety and may reach a size of 50cm (19in). It is confined to Australia, although sub-species are also seen on northern islands. These include the Triton (*C. g. triton*) and Blue-eyed (*C. g. ophthalmica*) forms, both of which have a naked area of blue skin surrounding the eyes, which is a deeper colour in the latter variety. All these races have much paler ear coverts than the Lesser Sulphur-crested Cockatoo.

The Umbrella (*C. alba*) and Moluccan Cockatoos (*C. moluccensis*) are two other large species, found in the Moluccan chain of islands. Umbrella Cockatoos are completely white, with a crest which is more in the shape of a hood, giving rise to their name. Their beaks are extremely powerful, moving one nineteenth century author to recommend that their aviaries should be built out of iron rods as used to cage lions! In some cases, they will even destroy thin chain-link fencing. The Moluccan Cockatoo is perhaps the most attractive member of the whole group, being pale pink with a red crest. These birds do have a very harsh call, which, coupled with the destructive capabilities of the previous species, will make them unsuitable for most people. They can, however, become quite tame and confiding, as exemplified by King Tut, now retired from Hollywood, but a well-loved film star of days gone by. He came to America in 1925, entertaining visitors at San Diego Zoo by dancing and singing up until his death in 1991.

Goffin's Cockatoo (*C. goffini*) has only been seen outside its native Tenimbar Islands since the early 1970s. These cockatoos, about the size of the Lesser Sulphur-crested have a relatively inconspicuous crest, and are predominantly white in colour with pale pink markings around the beak. They do not appear to make good pets, remaining shy, and given their very limited distribution, such birds should only be kept outside their natural habitat for breeding purposes. Once again, it was severe and widespread deforestation which resulted in Goffin's Cockatoos being exported in large numbers. Deprived of the forests on which they appear to depend, many would otherwise surely have died from starvation if they had not been despatched abroad.

The Bare-eyed Cockatoo or Little Corella (*C. sanguinea*) is very widespread in Australia, and will settle well as a pet, with some individuals proving quite good talkers. The Galah or Roseate Cockatoo (*Eolophus roseicapillus*), also common on this continent, has a relatively quieter voice than most other cockatoos. Birds of this species are pink with greyish wings and a white crest, and can become quite tame.

Macaws

These birds are found exclusively in Central and South America, and range in size from the Hyacinthine (*Anodorhynchus hyacinthinus*) which, at nearly 90 cm (3 ft), is the largest member of the whole parrot family, down to Hahn's Macaw (*A. nobilis*), barely one-third of this length. The striking appearance of many of the larger macaws makes them instantly appealing, but in reality, they should not be seriously considered as potential pets by most people. Their powerful beaks and harsh voices, apart from their size, make them unsuited to the majority of domestic environments.

The Blue and Gold Macaw (*Ara ararauna*) is probably better as a pet than the two Scarlet species. The Red and Yellow Macaw (*A. macao*) tends to be more aggressive than other species when it matures into breeding condition, whereas the Red and Green or Green-winged Macaw (*A. chloroptera*) is even larger, being about 2.5 cm (1 in) shorter than the Hyacinthine. This latter species is extremely expensive to purchase, but tame individuals are usually very gentle, which is certainly a trait to be encouraged in a bird whose beak can exert a calculated pressure of 300 lb per sq in.

All these species are becoming much scarcer in their native haunts, with the Red and Yellow Macaw now nearly extinct in Mexico, as a direct result of the clearance of the forest habitat. Another species occurring in this region, the Military Macaw (*A. militaris*) would also appear threatened. These macaws are relatively dull, being predominantly green with bluish flight feathers and a band of bright scarlet above the nostrils. In common with other species, the Military Macaw has a virtually naked area of skin extending from the eye to the lower beak.

Hyacinthine Macaw (*Anodorhynchus hyacinthinus*). The largest psittacine, reaching a length of nearly 90 cm (3 ft), whose beak can exert a pressure of 300 lb per sq in.

Dwarf Macaws comprise the smaller members of the genus, which also have basically green plumage. These, like their larger relatives, can be noisy, but usually become tame and may learn a few words, although they are not likely to prove fluent talkers. The Yellow-collared Macaw (*A. auricollis*) has been seen quite often in recent years, with a broad yellow band extending around the back of the neck. They are approximately 45 cm (18 in) in length, and occur in central South America, from Brazil to Argentina. Immature birds perhaps surprisingly have grey feet, which start turning pink from the age of three months onwards.

The Severe Macaw (*A. s. severa*) and the closely-related subspecies known as the Chestnut-fronted (*A. s. castaneifrons*), occur further north, ranging from eastern Panama down into Bolivia. Youngsters in this case can be recognized by their dark irides, which also serve to distinguish immatures of other species in the genus *Ara*. Severe Macaws have a chestnut band above the beak, and around the edge of bare facial skin either side of the lower beak. Red plumage occurs at the bend of the wings, and at the top of the legs.

Far right A Military Macaw (*Ara militaris*). One of the less colourful of the larger species of macaw.

Various other Dwarf Macaws may be encountered occasionally, of which Illiger's (*A. maracana*) is perhaps the most attractive, with a broad patch of red feathering between the legs, and again on the head. The Noble Macaw (*A. n. cumanensis*) is very similar to Hahn's Macaw, but can be distinguished by its yellowish upper mandible, which is completely black in the case of the latter species. Although not sexually dimorphic (like all macaws), these birds in particular have proved prolific in aviaries. Perhaps the most noteworthy breeding, however, concerns the recent success of a pair of Green-winged Macaws. They nested in their cage in the living room of the Franklin family, and had a single baby which hatched on Christmas Eve 1980, and thus was christened 'Noel'.

Mynah birds

There are various species of mynah birds offered for sale, but for a talking pet, only the Greater Hill variety (*Gracula r. religiosa*) should be considered. These command a much higher price than other species, such as the Common Mynah, (*Acridotheres tristis*), which, although they may become tame, never achieve any degree of talking prowess. The Lesser Hill Mynah (*G. r. intermedia*) is also not such a talented talker, being smaller than the Greater variety, with less prominent wattles.

The Greater Hill Mynah is approximately 25 cm (10 in) in length, with jet black glossy plumage, which can show various shades of irridescence, typically having a purplish sheen around the neck. There is an area of white in the flight feathers. An unusual feature is the wattles, which are yellow in a mature bird, and centred largely behind the eyes. The beak colour is somewhat variable, in view of the numerous recognized subspecies, but is of an orangish shade. These birds have a wide distribution in fact, being found over much of southern Asia, with the majority kept as pets originating in Thailand or India. The Javan subspecies (*G. r. javana*) is slightly larger with bigger wattles, and rarely available, but these birds are regarded by some as potentially the best talkers.

Young mynahs are sometimes known as 'gapers' because of their habit of begging for food, and will be much duller than an adult bird. Their wattles are paler, as well as being reduced in size, and only really develop from the age of a year onwards. They are most responsive to training at this earlier stage, however, and soon become confident in new surroundings. The vocabularies of mynahs may not be as large as those of some parrots, but their powers of mimicry are probably superior. Unfortunately, mynahs have a short lifespan, and rarely attain twenty years of age.

8 A few more exotic birds

While the previous chapters concentrated on species which are often available, and have relatively straightforward requirements, there are others that can make equally attractive pets, but often need more care. The colourful group of lories and lorikeets for example, require nectar as the basis of their diet, supplemented with a selection of fruit, either tinned or fresh, as well as a little dried seed. Their relatively fluid droppings are likely to prove a further drawback in the home.

These birds do, however, have very playful natures, apart from their bright coloration, and can learn to talk successfully in some cases. A hand-reared Black-capped Lory (*Domicella lory*) bred at the Naples Zoological Gardens in Italy soon learned to talk, without being specifically taught. This bird has also proved a talented mimic, being able to reproduce the sound of a ringing telephone, followed by the comment 'Director not here'! Another pair of this species barked like a dog at regular intervals as well as copying the calls of seagulls and chickens. These lories do have a loud call, which may well prove disturbing when they are kept indoors. The plumage of this species is a mixture of red and blue, with a black cap on the head. Youngsters can be recognized by their horn-coloured bills, which become orange when they mature.

Eclectus parrots can settle well in a domestic environment, providing they have an opportunity to fly regularly, preferably in a flight. These birds provide the most extreme example of sexual dimorphism in psittacines. When they were first discovered it was believed that cocks, with their green plumage, were a different species from hens, which are largely red in colour. Cocks generally prove better pets than hens, which are more aggressive, but they never become proficient talkers or mimics. A number are hand-reared each year, however, and young birds have dark irides, while their beaks are brown rather than orange-red.

Caiques, which are small parrots from South America, also become very tame, as well as mischievous, when kept as pets. It is preferable to keep these companionable birds in pairs, rather than individually. The Black-headed form (*Pionites*

Above Black-capped Lories (*Domicella lory*) may learn to say a few words.

Above right Eclectus provide the most extreme example of sexual dimorphism. The hen is shown here, whereas the cock is predominantly green in colour.

Right A Black-headed Caique (*Pionites melanocephala*).

Far right A Pekin Robin (*Leiothrix lutea*). These active birds are quite attractive songsters.

melanocephala) can be distinguished from the White-breasted (*P. leucogaster*) by the difference in head coloration. The black seen in the case of the former species is replaced by orange in the latter instance. Various subspecies are also recognized. These birds must always have fresh twigs to chew, as they are naturally destructive, apart from being noisy.

The Hanging Parrots (*Loriculus* species), named after their unusual habit of roosting upside down, are found throughout most of south-east Asia. Although they do not talk, they will thrive alongside finches in a planted flight, given a diet of nectar, fruit and small seeds. The Blue-crowned species (*L. galgulus*) is perhaps the most attractive, being only 12 cm (5 in) in length. Hens can be recognized as they lack the red feathering present under the chin of cocks. Pairs may even breed given a small nestbox and suitable material, which hens carry to the box tucked in amongst their body feathering. The eggs are brooded for approximately twenty days before hatching, and the young fledge when nearly five weeks old.

A variety of other nectar-feeding birds can be kept in suitable planted flights. The Pekin Robin (*Leiothrix lutea*) will take fruit coated with an insectivorous mixture, as well as mealworms. These birds should not be kept in a mixed collection, because they have a tendency to steal both eggs and chicks from breeding pairs of other species. They can become quite tame, taking mealworms from the hand, and have an attractive voice, giving rise to their other name of Pekin Nightingale.

Another species sometimes encountered which has an attractive, lively disposition is the Yuhina, or Flowerpecker, of which the Black-chinned form (*Yuhina nigramenta*) is most commonly available. Females can be recognized because they possess smaller crests, with more widespread red markings on the beak. They do best if kept in pairs in planted flights, as with all these birds, but are aggressive to other members of their own kind.

The South American Sugar Birds and Tanagers are two related groups and include some of the most colourful softbills occurring on this continent. They should be kept only in flights, however, and never cages. The Purple Sugar Bird (*Cyanerpes caeruleus*) may superficially resemble a hummingbird, with its narrow beak and vivid purple plumage in the case of the cock. They require nectar, and fruit cut into very small pieces, coated with an insectivorous mixture, as well as small insects. Like Tanagers, these birds also enjoy soaked mynah pellets and are able to break off small pieces. Wholemeal bread, soaked as described earlier, can be given daily as an alternative. Cocks often fight viciously in spite of their size, and so should not be kept together.

The larger species of Tanager, such as the Mountain, are aggressive, and should be kept apart from other birds. The smaller Euphonias, which are all about 10 cm (4 in) in length are relatively easy to establish, and can be sexed, hens being duller. The *Tangara* species, such as the Paradise (*T. chilensis*) are extremely colourful in some cases, with a weak metallic-sounding song, and often become quite tame. For those who are interested in acquiring such birds, reference should be made to a more specialized text before purchasing them, so that their detailed requirements can be fully appreciated.

The toucans are another family occurring exclusively in Central and South America. While genuine youngsters can become delightfully tame but cannot talk, adults will remain wild, and never settle well as pets. The Aracaris are preferable to the smaller toucanets, such as the Emerald, which often prove extremely nervous. Most larger toucans cannot be housed satisfactorily in the average home, as they must be given adequate flying space to prevent them becoming over-weight. They do well on a diet of mynah pellets and mixed fruits, coated with an insectivorous mixture, as well as meal-worms and a small daily ration of lean minced beef.

Seedeaters

The Diamond Dove (*Geopelia cuneata*) is an attractive member of a mixed flight, and unlike larger species, does not fly about wildly, at the risk of scalping itself. They are about 19 cm ($7\frac{1}{2}$ in) in length, and cocks can be distinguished, at least during the breeding season, by broader and more prominent circles of red skin around the eyes. These doves build a nest in a canary nest-pan, but once the chicks have fledged, they must be removed immediately because they are likely to be attacked by their parents. Mutations such as the Silver, which is a paler form of the normal grey, are now becoming more widespread.

A similar mutation has occurred in the case of the small Chinese Painted Quail (*Excalfactoria chinensis*), which is only about 11.5 cm ($4\frac{1}{2}$ in) in size. These birds live happily on the floor of a flight, but cocks do have a tendency to persecute their mates, which are always more expensive. Each cock should be kept separate in a flight with two, if not three females. The hens will often lay on the floor of a flight, but may not incubate the eggs. If chicks do hatch, they can escape through the tiniest gap, in view of their small size. Egg-food must be available when there is a brood of chicks, as they will often take this in preference to seed at first.

There are various weavers which are not really suitable for keeping indoors, because they never become tame, nor are

Left A Yellow-naped Yuhina (*Yuhina flavicollis*). Various species are available, and all have similar requirements.

Above Diamond Doves (*Geopelia cuneata*) usually breed readily if given a canary nest pan to support their nest.

Above right The Blue-crowned Hanging Parrot (*Loriculus galgullus*) requires fruit and nectar as a significant part of its diet.

Right Tanagers as a group are often referred to as living gems because of the dazzling beauty of their plumage. Over two hundred species are recognized.

Below A cock Yellow-legged Sugar Bird (*Cyanerpes caeruleus chocoana*) or Honeycreeper.

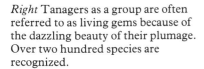

likely to breed. In addition, they prove generally aggressive, and should never be kept with small finches. Weavers, as their name suggests, do have the interesting habit of making nests, given adequate material, and these are often suspended from the roof of their flight. Whydahs also occur in Africa, with cocks developing magnificent tail plumes when in breeding condition, and are thus referred to as IFC (in full colour), compared to OOC (out of colour). They are most unlikely to raise chicks indoors, if kept in individual pairs. Some species are parasitic, laying in the nests of specific waxbills. They only show to good advantage when housed in flights of 450 cm (15 ft) in length. Each cock naturally acquires a harem comprised of ten or more hens, and will only breed successfully when given such numbers in suitable planted surroundings.

Index